INTERNATIONAL JOURNAL OF PSYCHOLOGY, 1998, *33* (3), 185–189

The Neuropsychology of Consciousness: The Mind–Body Problem Re-addressed

Kurt Pawlik

University of Hamburg, Germany

In this introductory contribution by the convenor of the 1996 Invited Presidential Symposium at the XXVI International Congress of Psychology, the recent renaissance of psychological, especially neuro-psychological research into components and processes of consciousness is briefly reviewed. Conceptual dimensions of "consciousness" are distinguished, with an emphasis on consciousness in the sense of awareness, wakefulness, and control of overt behaviour, which are also central concepts in the subsequent symposium contributions.

Dans cette introduction au Symposium du Président tenu lors du XXVI Congrès International de Psychologie, l'auteur passe brièvement en revue les recherches sur les composantes et les processus de la conscience qui ont connu récemment une renaissance en psychologie et plus particulièrement, en neuropsychologie. Il distingue les dimensions conceptuelles de la conscience, en mettant l' accent sur la prise de conscience, l'éveil et le contrôle du comportement observable qui constituent des concepts centraux dans les contributions ultérieures au symposium.

When reflecting on the choice of topic for the 1996 Invited Presidential Symposium at the XXVI International Congress of Psychology in Montréal, Canada, my preference readily converged on *the* number one basic problem field currently attracting experimental and theoretical psychologists and neuroscientists alike: the conceptual nature and structural basis of human consciousness. So I chose "The Neuropsychology of Consciousness" as the theme for the symposium. In cooperation with the International Brain Research Organization and in the context of the Human Brain Project of the International Council of Scientific Unions, the symposium should bring together high-ranking research specialists from the contributing scientific disciplines. I was delighted that Professors Masao Ito, Wako, Japan, Past President of the International Brain Research Organization and President of the International Union of Physiological Science, Rodolfo Llinas, neuroscientist at the New York University Medical Center, USA,

Hellmuth Petsche, neurophysiologist at the University of Vienna, Austria, Karl H. Pribram, neurosurgeon and experimental neuropsychologist at Radford University, USA, and Lorenz W. Weiskrantz, experimental neuropsychologist at Oxford University, UK, all agreed to participate. One invitee, Professor Ernest Hilgard, experimental psychologist at Stanford University, USA, unfortunately was unable to take part. In sending his warm regards, Hilgard called it a truly "wise choice" to devote the 1996 IUPsyS Presidential Symposium to the neuropsychological study of consciousness.

The contributions to this Topical Section of the *International Journal of Psychology* are revised and expanded versions of the presentations at the Montréal Presidential Symposium[1]. In the present introductory contribution the recent renaissance of consciousness as a legitimate psychological construct is briefly reviewed, with synoptic reference to current research literature and research approaches.

Requests for reprints should be addressed to K. Pawlik, Psychologisches Institut 1, Von Melle Park 11, 20146 Hamburg, Germany. Fax: +49 40 4123 6551. E-mail:pawlik@rrz.uni-hamburg.de

[1] Regrettably R. Llinas could not complete his part for this issue.

CONSCIOUSNESS: THE FALL AND RISE OF A SCIENTIFIC CONSTRUCT

The November 1992 issue of the magazine *Discover* lists "*What is consciousness?*" among the 10 greatest, most challenging, and still unresolved questions in science today. Similarly, in a scientific session at the 1996 General Assembly of the International Council of Scientific Unions in Washington DC, the Nobel Laureate physicist L.M. Lederman highlighted the unravelling of human consciousness as a top-priority issue of modern-day scientific enquiry. And F. Crick, British physicist/biochemist and recipient, together with J.D. Watson, of the Nobel Prize for their discovery of the molecular structure of deoxyribonucleic acid (DNA), devoted his recent and widely acclaimed book to the "astonishing hypothesis" pursued in research on consciousness (Crick, 1994).

Indeed, research into the nature, structural basis, and process nature of consciousness has become a "hot" topic in present-day theoretical and experimental psychology, in clinical and experimental neuropsychology, in neuroscience, in cognitive science, and in philosophy at large. In recent years, particularly since the early 1990s, an ever-growing number of profound texts and edited volumes have been published that deal with empirical research and theoretical issues pertaining to human consciousness. Examples are Baars (1997), Chalmers (1996), P.M. Churchland (1996), Dennett (1991), Flanagan (1995), Hameroff, Kaszniak, and Scott (1996), Ito, Miyashita, and Rolls (1997), Llinas and Churchland (1996), Umiltá (1994), and Weiskrantz (1997). This crop of publications is augmented, for example, by the large section on consciousness (Schacter, 1996) in the encyclopaedic coverage of cognitive neurosciences by Gazzaniga (1996), by a number of specialized new journals (for example: Bears, Banks, & McGovern, 1992–; Goguen, Forman, & Sutherland, 1994–; Hameroff, Kaszniak, Laukes, & Scott, 1997), by numerous special journal issues (for example, Burri & Perrig, 1997), and by special workshops like the recent satellite symposium *Can neuroscience explain consciousness?*, organized by Chalmers and Kaszniak at the 1997 Society for Neuroscience Meeting in New Orleans, USA. And attention to research into consciousness is likely to increase still further.

This signals a turn in the conceptual history of psychology and of the behavioural sciences at large. Interestingly enough, and from an historical perspective, "consciousness" has not been a target object of early classical Western philosophical thinking (cf. Wilkes, 1988). It was not until Descartes, some 350 years ago, that the "mind" (in the sense of thinking self-awareness; "Meditationes", 1641) got introduced as a topic of philosophical reflection. Rooted in the Cartesian ontological tradition, generations of philosophers since have proposed any number of monistic and dualistic (up to trialistic) "solutions" to the so-called mind–body problem: how "immaterial" mind, how mental states and subjective experience may be part of, evolve from, interact, or co-exist with bodily processes. In this paper and the following contributions to this Topical Section little attention, if any, will be given to the philosophical treatment of this mind–body problem (see, for example, P.S. Churchland, 1986; Bieri, 1993, for modern accounts in terms of emergence theory and analytical philosophy). In a more modest (and heuristically more operative?) approach, the emphasis in this issue is on the analysis of neuropsychological correlates rather than on ontological roots of human conscious experience (see also Chalmers, 1996, for a recent and ambitious presentation of this distinction).

In its early days as a distinct new discipline, psychology still included consciousness in the definition of its object of study. For instance, Volume 1 of William James' famous *The principles of psychology* starts out (1890, p. 1) with the statement:

> Psychology is the Science of Mental Life, both of its phenomena and their conditions. The phenomena are such things as we call feelings, desires, cognitions, reasonings, decisions, and the like; and, superficially considered, their variety and complexity is such as to leave a chaotic impression on the observer

to continue a few pages later (op. cit., p. 4):

> . . . if the brain be injured, consciousness is abolished or altered, even although every other organ in the body may be ready to play its normal part. . . . The fact that the brain is the one immediate bodily condition of the mental operations is indeed so universally admitted nowadays that I need spend no more time in illustrating it . . .

Similar definitions of the object of study of psychological science can be quoted from many authors of that time. As every first-year student of psychology will be taught, in the decades to follow consciousness and subjective mental phenomena became more and more excluded from psychology, most notably in North America, both as a field of research and as a resource or target of theory development. Behaviourism stayed away from mental phenomena deliberately for reasons of methodology, of theoretical parsimony, or both. By the middle of this century, mental phenomena and consciousness continued to play a role in teaching and research only in a minority of university departments of psychology, most notably in continental Europe (see, for example, Luria, 1966, Rohracher, 1946). In this way, students of psychology at some continental European universities (including the present author!) still had the benefit of being trained to conceive of psychology as the science of behaviour *and* conscious subjective experience. In the psychological world at large, however, as has been pointed out by Searle (1992), it took until the 1960s and early 1970s for consciousness to become "rediscovered" as a "respectable, useful and probably necessary" target of psychological enquiry (Mandler, 1975; see also Natsoulas, 1978). Looking back on this development, Searle (1992) observed rightly:

> As recently as a few years ago, if one raised the subject of consciousness in cognitive science discussions, it was generally regarded as a form of bad taste, and graduate students, who are always attuned to the social mores of their disciplines, would roll their eyes at the ceiling and assume expressions of mild disgust.

What are the developments, scientific, methodological, or other, that gave rise to this change of perspective in psychology, as shown in the recent wealth of research and publications on consciousness referred to earlier? We can identify at least four broader scientific developments that seem to contribute to this change of perspective and to the increasing interest other disciplines too are taking in mental phenomena and consciousness today. These are:

1. the emergence of *cognitive science* as the cross-disciplinary study of information processing, artificial intelligence and computational models of mental functioning (cf. Gazzaniga, 1996);

2. the rapid growth of *neuroscience methodology* for studying nervous system correlates of changes in mental state, of mental and behavioural performance, and of different states of awareness and wakefulness (cf. Kandel, Schwartz, & Jessell, 1995) (coherence-analytic electroencephalographic techniques, functional brain imaging techniques, particularly functional magnetic resonance imaging or fMRI);

3. the development of *psychological methodology* for studying verbal self-reports, expressive movements, and the temporal microstructure of changes in behavioural flow as correlates of variations in mental state (cf. Buse & Pawlik, 1996); and

4. advances in *clinical neuropsychology* in the assessment of pathological variations in mental state, in wakefulness vs. coma, and in improved psychometric assessments of these variations (cf. Lezak, 1995) and in cognitive behaviour therapy (cf. Grawe, Donati, & Bernauer, 1994).

At the time of this writing, we are still at the beginning of taking advantage of potential synergies from these developments, in methodological terms and in theoretical respects, and in a preparatory state for interdisciplinary research on human consciousness and mental phenomena, as will be illustrated in the contributions to this Topical Section.

DIMENSIONS OF CONSCIOUSNESS

The term consciousness is used in different ways and with different meanings. Authors either concentrate on *functional* aspects of consciousness, in the sense of attention and awareness, or on *phenomenological* aspects of consciousness, in the sense of self-awareness and self-consciousness (i.e. internal awareness of one's own conscious experiences) (see also Natsoulas, 1978; Shallice, 1972). Johnson-Laird (1988) proposed to distinguish between four process functions of consciousness: awareness; control (of overt behaviour); self-awareness; and intentions (as underlying purposive behaviour). A frequently quoted taxonomy of definitions of consciousness goes back to Bisiach (1988), who drew a distinction between three different conceptualizations:

1. consciousness C1: referring to a person's ability to have awareness of his/her subjective experiences, his/her ability to perceive variations in mental state (consciousness in the strict sense of the term);

2. consciousness C2: referring to the access which this awareness system can take to some

or many of its parts, to its own mental processes (consciousness in the sense of awareness); and

3. consciousness C3: referring to a nonphysical entity in the sense of an "immaterial mind" (*sensu* Descartes).

C3 conceptualizations obviously fall beyond limits of empirical scientific enquiry, and the majority of consciousness research concentrates on C2 data.

In the study of the neuropsychology of consciousness one wishes to identify structural or procedural neurocorrelates of variations in C1 and C2 data, that is of variations in wakefulness, in awareness and control of overt behaviour, and in subjective self-awareness. As readers may easily verify from the literature referenced in the previous section, no fewer than 50 or so neuropsychological "explanations" have been proposed for different components of consciousness (see also Hirst, 1996). Diametrically opposing views have been held, for example, by Gazzaniga (1988), according to whom awareness is but a property of neural networks per se, and Umiltá (1988), who identifies consciousness with a central brain processor of limited capacity that controls cognitive processes, with self-awareness being a necessary condition for this control system to become effectively operative. In search for a central processor, a range of neuronal candidate correlates of awareness and cognitive control have been hypothesized, including special forebrain structures, transient synchronization of neuron discharge patterns, or thalomocortical coherence functions (see also Llinas & Churchland, 1996, for these and other proposed psychophysical "bridging principles").

Contributions to this Topical Section introduce research strategies in delineating neuronal correlates of consciousness functions, and in identifying critical neuronal subsystems and process characteristics essential for the maintainance of functions of consciousness. They are presented here in the form submitted by the symposium participants, without attempts towards premature integration. The contributions concentrate on the neuropsychology of consciousness in the sense of wakefulness and awareness, the two functions of consciousness most readily open to experimental study.

I hope that the publication of these symposium contributions will further encourage and stimulate experimental psychological, particularly neuropsychological, study of consciousness

and of mental phenomena, at the same time highlighting what has become an emerging consensus in the discussion section of the Montréal Congress Presidential Symposium: that, as an enquiry into the human mind, the neuropsychological study of consciousness is far from being reductive in methodological or theoretical terms, and opens up new levels of promising interdisciplinarity in the behavioural sciences and neurosciences.

REFERENCES

Baars, B.J. (1997). *In the theater of consciousness.* Oxford: Oxford University Press.

Bears, B.J., Banks, W.P., & McGovern, K. (Eds.). (1992–). *Consciousness and cognition.* New York: Academic Press.

Bieri, P. (1993). *Analytische Philosophie des Geistes* (2nd edn.). [Analytical philosophy of the mind.] Bodenheim, Germany: Hain.

Bisiach, E. (1988). The (haunted) brain and consciousness. In A.J. Marcel & E. Bisiach (Eds.), *Consciousness in contemporary science* (pp. 101–120). Oxford: Oxford University Press.

Burri, S., & Perrig, W. (Eds.). (1997). Kognition und Bewußtsein. [Cognition and consciousness.] Special Issue: *Sprache und Kognition, 16,* 133–210.

Buse, L., & Pawlik, K. (1996). Ambulatory behavioral assessment and in-field performance testing. In J. Fahrenberg & M. Myrtek (Eds.), *Ambulatory assessment* (pp. 29–50). Göttingen, Germany: Hogrefe.

Chalmers, D.J. (1996). *The conscious mind.* Oxford: Oxford University Press.

Churchland, P.M. (1996). *Matter and consciousness* (2nd edn.). Cambridge, MA: MIT Press.

Churchland, P.S. (1986). *Neurophilosophy.* Cambridge, MA: MIT Press.

Crick, F. (1994). *The astonishing hypothesis.* New York: Simon & Schuster.

Dennett, D.C. (1991). *Consciousness explained.* Boston, MA: Little Brown.

Flanagan, C.P. (1995). *Consciousness reconsidered.* Cambridge, MA: MIT Press.

Gazzaniga, M.S. (1988). Brain modularity: Towards a philosophy of conscious experience. In A.J. Marcel & E. Bisiach (Eds.), *Consciousness in contemporary science* (pp. 218–238). Oxford: Oxford University Press.

Gazzaniga, M.S. (Editor-in-Chief). (1996). *The cognitive neurosciences.* Cambridge, MA: MIT Press.

Goguen, J.A., Forman, K.C., & Sutherland, K. (Eds.). (1994–). *Journal of consciousness studies.* Thorverton, UK: Imprint Academic.

Grawe, K., Donati, R., & Bernauer, F. (1994). *Psychotherapie im Wandel.* [Psychotherapy undergoing change.] Göttingen, Germany: Hogrefe.

Hameroff, S.R., Kaszniak, A.W., Laukes, J., & Scott, A.C. (1997). *Consciousness bulletin.* Tucson, AZ: University of Arizona.

Hameroff, S.R., Kaszniak, A.W., & Scott, A.C. (Eds.).

(1996). *Toward a science of consciousness.* Cambridge, MA: MIT Press.

Hirst, W. (1996). Cognitive aspects of consciousness. In M.S. Gazzaniga (Editor-in-Chief), *The cognitive neurosciences* (pp. 1307–1319). Cambridge, MA: MIT Press.

Ito, M., Miyashita, Y., & Rolls, E.T. (Eds.). (1997). *Cognition, computation, and consciousness.* Oxford: Oxford University Press.

James, W. (1890). *The principles of psychology. Vol. 1.* New York: Holt.

Johnson-Laird, P.N. (1988). *The computer and the mind: An introduction to cognitive science.* Cambridge, MA: Harvard University Press.

Kandel, E.R., Schwartz, J.H., & Jessell, T.M. (Eds.). (1995). *Essentials of neural science and behavior.* Norwalk, CT: Appleton & Lange.

Lezak, M.D. (1995). *Neuropsychological assessment* (3rd edn.). New York: Oxford University Press.

Llinas, R., & Churchland, P.S. (Eds.). (1996). *The mind-brain continuum: Sensory processes.* Cambridge, MA: MIT Press.

Luria, A.R. (1966). Brain and mind. *Soviet Psychology and Psychiatry, 4*(3–4), 62–69.

Mandler, G. (1975). Consciousness: Respectable, useful, and probably necessary. In R. Solso (Ed.), *Information processing and cognition: The Loyola Symposium* (pp. 229–254). Hillsdale, NJ: Lawrence Erlbaum Associates Inc.

Natsoulas, T. (1978). Consciousness. *American Psychologist, 33,* 906–914.

Rohracher, H. (1946). *Einführung in die Psychologie.* [Introduction to psychology.] Vienna: Urban & Schwarzenberg.

Rychlak, J.F. (1997). *In defense of human consciousness.* Washington, DC: American Psychological Association.

Schacter, D.L. (Section Editor). (1996). Consciousness. In M.S. Gazzaniga (Editor-in-Chief), *The cognitive neurosciences* (pp. 1291–1400). Cambridge, MA: MIT Press.

Searle, J.R. (1992). *The rediscovery of the mind.* Cambridge, MA: MIT Press.

Shallice, T. (1972). Dual functions of consciousness. *Psychological Review, 79,* 383–393.

Umiltá, C. (1988). The control operations of consciousness. In A.J. Marcel & E. Bisiach (Eds.), *Consciousness in contemporary science* (pp. 334–356). Oxford: Oxford University Press.

Umiltá, C. (Ed.). (1994). *Attention and performance. XV. Consciousness and nonconscious information processing.* Cambridge, MA: MIT Press.

Weiskrantz, L. (1997). *Consciousness lost and found.* Oxford: Oxford University Press.

Wilkes, K.V. (1988). -, yíshí, duh, um, and consciousness. In A.J. Marcel & E. Bisiach (Eds.), *Consciousness in contemporary science* (pp. 16–41). Oxford: Oxford University Press.

INTERNATIONAL JOURNAL OF PSYCHOLOGY, 1998, *33* (3), 191–197

Consciousness from the Viewpoint of the Structural-functional Relationships of the Brain

Masao Ito

Brain Science Institute, RIKEN, Saitama, Japan

The brain of vertebrates consists of brainstem and spinal cord conducting reflexes, compound movements, and innate behaviour, and the cerebral neocortex generating sensorimotor function and association function. These five major functions are assisted by four regulatory systems: limbic system, basal ganglia, cerebellum and sleep-wakefulness brainstem centres. Consciousness contains three different levels, i.e., wakefulness, awareness and self-consciousness. Wakefulness is a fundamental brain function regulated by the brainstem wakefulness centres. Awareness represents integration of diverse sensory signals, largely in the neocortex, for the perception of what is going on in the external world. Consciousness in humans is directed to the self so that an individual is aware of what is going on in his or her internal world, i.e., the mind, and seems to be inherent to the association cortex, in particular the frontal lobe. Freud's id emerges from the hypothalamus and limbic system, whereas the ego involves both the sensorimotor and association cortices. The super-ego is likely to be embodied in part of the association cortex. When movement and thought are conceived as a control system function, instruction for control corresponds to the will which initiates these actions and which represents a positive aspect of consciousness. Though consciousness is related to brain structures in these ways, a crucial question remains as to how we subjectively experience will, affect or self-consciousness as a consequence of neuronal activities in the brain structures.

Le cerveau des vertébrés comprend le tronc cérébral et la moelle épinière qui servent de substrat aux réflexes, aux mouvements composés et au comportement inné, ainsi que le néocortex cérébral qui est responsable de la fonction sensori-motrice et de la fonction associative. Ces cinq fonctions principales sont assistées par quatre systèmes de régulation: le système limbique, les ganglions de la base, le cervelet et les centres d'éveil et du sommeil dans le tronc cérébral. Il y a trois niveaux de conscience: l'éveil, la prise de conscience et la conscience de soi. L'éveil est une fonction cérébrale fondamentale qui est contrôlée par les centres d'éveil du tronc cérébral. La prise de conscience représente l'intégration de divers signaux sensoriels, principalement dans le néocortex, qui permet de percevoir ce qui se passe dans l'environnement externe. Chez les humains, la conscience est tournée vers le soi de sorte qu'une personne prend conscience de ce qui se passe dans son monde interne, c'est-à-dire dans son esprit; la conscience semble relever du cortex associatif, en particulier du lobe frontal. Le Ça freudien émerge de l'hypothalamus et du système limbique alors que le Moi s'appuie sur les cortex sensori-moteur et associatif. Le Surmoi relèverait de certaines régions du cortex associatif. Si le mouvement et la pensée sont conçues comme la fonction d'un système de contrôle, une commande de contrôle correspond alors à la volonté qui amorce ces actions et qui représente un aspect positif de la conscience. Bien que l'on puisse ainsi relier la conscience à ces structures cérébrales, une question fondamentale demeure, à savoir comment les activités neurales dans ces structures donnent naissance à l'experience subjective de la volonté, de l'affect ou de la conscience de soi.

INTRODUCTION

The mechanisms underlying brain functions are difficult to elucidate, yet recent advances in neuroscience create optimistic expectations that these mechanisms may soon be explained. It is important to realize, however, that the mind encompasses a number of components such as perception, emotion, learning, thought, language, and awareness, as classified psychologically.

Requests for reprints should be addressed to Masao Ito, Brain Science Institute, RIKEN, Wako, Saitamo 351–01, Japan.

These components are related to certain distinct areas of the brain, and it is therefore possible to elucidate their mechanisms by identifying these areas and studying neural events taking place in them. In fact, an increasing number of these components have been topics of recent neuroscience research. Nevertheless, consciousness remains the most intriguing component for which related brain areas have not been clearly defined and consequently the adoption of an effective neuroscience approach is difficult. Despite this difficulty, interest in consciousness is expanding among neuroscientists. This article examines the problems of understanding consciousness from the viewpoints of structural-functional relationships in the brain. The basic structural-functional relationships in the brain and their evolutionary development will first be outlined and their relevance to consciousness will then be discussed from psychological, psychoanalytical, control, and computational aspects.

FUNCTIONAL ORGANIZATION OF THE BRAIN

In the lower vertebrates such as fish, frogs, and snakes, the brainstem and spinal cord control three categories of functions. These are (1) various reflexes, (2) compound movements such as locomotion and saccadic eye movement, and (3) innate behaviour such as food intake, drinking, and reproductive behaviour. The centre for innate behaviour is located in the hypothalamus at the rostral end of the brainstem, whereas centres for reflexes and compound movements are distributed throughout the spinal cord, medulla oblongata, and midbrain. The combinations of these three types of functions account for most of the behaviours of lower vertebrates. However, these functions are all mechanistic and stereotyped in nature, and they alone would not be sufficient to secure an animal's survival. For this reason, four other structures appear to be indispensable for survival: (A) the limbic system, (B) the basal ganglia, (C) the cerebellum, and (D) the sleep-wakefulness centres in the brainstem.

The limbic system is an evolutionarily old part of the cerebrum and acts to modify innate behaviours by positive and negative reinforcement. For example, a rat that perceives water to be sweet will continue drinking, whereas a rat perceiving the same water to be salty will avoid it. This behaviour toward the same water is thus reinforced positively or negatively due to tasting experiences so that its purposefulness for animals' survival is maintained. The role of the limbic system can be defined as conferring purposefulness on innate behaviours.

The basal ganglia form a massive network lying in the deep interior of the cerebrum. Even though it is still a matter under debate, the major function of the basal ganglia seems to be the following. Since numerous activities, competitive or even conflicting, may occur in the brainstem and spinal cord simultaneously, a mechanism of choosing one among them and suppressing the others is necessary for the stable operation of the functional systems. My proposal is that the basal ganglia, by such selection, ensures this stability.

The adaptive mechanisms of the cerebellum have been well defined (Ito, 1984). A small compartment of the cerebellum forms an adaptive unit that changes its input-output relationships through learning driven by error signals. A type of synaptic plasticity called long-term depression, LTD, is the major mechanism of this error-driven learning (Ito, 1993). For example, when an animal's locomotion on a treadmill is perturbed by a sudden change of the speed for one limb, the locomotion initially becomes irregular, but the cerebellar adaptive unit connected to the locomotion system acts to modify parameters of locomotion by referring to the errors forwarded through spinocerebellar pathways so that the animal's stable locomotion is restored (Yanagihara & Kondo, 1996).

The sleep-wakefulness centres in the brainstem may exert a more general action than the other regulatory systems upon the functional systems (1)–(3), such as the resting and recovery during sleep from the exhaustion caused during waking activities. In view of the neuroscientific data accumulated to date, it is reasonable to assume that the three functional systems (1)–(3) and four regulatory systems (A)–(D) together form the major part of the central nervous system of lower vertebrates and account for their behaviours.

ORGANIZATION IN MAMMALIAN AND PRIMATE BRAINS

In lower mammals such as rats, cats, and dogs, the cerebral neocortex develops and constitutes a fourth functional system in the brain. This fourth system consists of the sensory and perisensory areas of the neocortex as well as the underlying thalamus. Both sensory and perisensory areas are represented in the parieto-latero-occipital lobe.

The sensory information processed in the cerebral cortex is utilized as inputs to reflexes, compound movements, or innate behaviour, but it is the major input to the motor area of the neocortex that generates command signals of movements to be sent to the skeletomuscular system. The motor cortex is linked with the premotor and supplementary motor areas, which programme movements. The fourth functional system in the cerebral cortex carries out elaborate sensorimotor functions. My hypothesis is that the four regulatory systems (A)–(D) act upon this fourth functional system similarly to the functional systems (1)–(3), with basically the same operational principles.

In primates, the association cortex has developed to such an extent that in humans it occupies two thirds of the entire cerebral neocortex, and together with the associated part of the thalamus, constitutes a fifth functional system in the brain. The primate association cortex has two major areas, i.e. the prefrontal area anterior to the motor and premotor areas and the parietolateral area surrounded by the primary sensory areas. The parietolateral area collects sensory information from various sensory and perisensory areas, and integrates this information to form images and concepts or ideas. The prefrontal area sends command signals to the sensorimotor cortex to interfere with the fourth functional system as in the case of attention (Roland, 1981) or no-go suppression (Sasaki, Gemba, Nambu, & Matsuzaki, 1993). The prefrontal area also sends command signals to the parietolateral area. The unique feature of the fifth functional system is that the prefrontal and parietolateral areas are interconnected to form an internal loop in the brain. The prefrontal cortex acts to manipulate images, concepts, and ideas encoded in the parietolateral area via this loop, and this loop action seems to represent the process of thought. The fifth functional system should also be under the influence of the four regulatory systems (A)–(D) (Ito, 1997).

WAKEFULNESS, AWARENESS, AND SELF-CONSCIOUSNESS

Consciousness has been considered in neuroscience in connection with three different categories of brain functions: wakefulness, awareness, and self-consciousness. These functions could be related to different divisions of the brain as described earlier.

Wakefulness, as the opposite of sleep, is the most fundamental brain function common to all vertebrates from fish to humans, as represented by regulatory system (D). A number of structures in the brainstem have been shown to be involved in sleep-wakefulness, and an unexpected recent finding by Hayaishi's group (Urade et al., 1993) is that the chorioid plexus is an essential link in the brain pathway that leads to sleep induction. However, it is still unclear what is the actual initial event leading to sleep induction, and what is the final event that is linked to consciousness. Even though we have a fairly concrete view of the brainstem system controlling sleep-wakefulness, there is as yet no clear understanding regarding the input or output of this system.

Awareness is related to a cerebral cortical process for the perception of what is going on in the external world. This process has recently been considered in terms of the so-called binding problem (Crick & Koch, 1990). When a human sees an object, its properties such as form, colour, and movement are processed in separate areas of the visual association cortex, as has been revealed in recent neuroscientific studies. Yet, the individual senses all of these properties at once and recognizes the object as having these properties in union. There has been considerable debate as to whether this integration occurs due to functional resonance between separate areas of the cerebral cortex, or due to convergence through anatomical pathways from these areas to another level of the brain, but no clear conclusion has yet been drawn. Nevertheless, the binding problem is inherent to cognitive processes in the fourth functional system, and could be common to mammalian brains.

Consciousness in humans is directed to the self so that an individual is aware of what is going on in his or her internal world, i.e. the mind. Self-consciousness implies monitoring of what the self is doing, giving rise to the perception of self. The ability to recognize oneself in a mirror is often taken as evidence of the existence of self-consciousness. Since a chimpanzee can learn to do this (Gallup, 1985), self-consciousness may not be unique to humans, and may be common, to a greater or lesser degree, to primates who possess a well-developed association cortex. However, the functional localization of self-consciousness is unclear, which makes finding an approach suitable to the elucidation of the neural mechanisms involved extremely difficult. In view of evolution, self-consciousness could be inherent to the fifth functional system of the brain. In fact, a lesion of the human right frontal lobe from its surrounding areas has been reported to impair the perception of self (Stuss, Picton, & Alexander, in press). Because of the recent development of imaging techniques for mapping human brain activities, identification of the functional localization for self-consciousness will be a challenging problem in neuroscientific research.

ID, EGO, AND SUPER-EGO

A psychoanalytical theory developed by Freud (1923) is that the self consists of three components: id, ego and super-ego. Id is an English translation of *es* in German meaning it, and implies the most primitive component of the self, which generates biological, instinctive drives for the pursuit of pleasure. By contrast, ego interacts with the external world and rationally controls the id in order to make life orderly and productive, and in harmony with the actual world. Super-ego represents the cultural, moral, and ethical components of the self, which act to supervise the id and ego. Freud (1923) explained human behaviours based on the mechanics of interaction among these three components of the self. Conflicts among them can lead to neurotic disorders. Freud (1923) assumed that the id and the super-ego, and even a large part of the ego, operate subconsciously below the threshold of attention, yet these subconscious mental processes play important roles in determining human behaviour.

In the hierarchical organization of the brain just described, the id seems to involve the hypothalamus and limbic system. Since the id predominates in babies, the neocortex, which is still immature in babies, is excluded as a functional localization of id. The limbic system contains the amygdala, which is the structure for evaluating whether stimuli are favourable or unfavourable for the survival of an animal. Those stimuli judged as favourable will induce pleasant emotions in the hypothalamus that drive the animal to approach the stimuli. By contrast, those stimuli judged as unfavourable will induce anger or fear in the hypothalamus and thereby evoke attack or flee behaviour. The limbic system also includes the anterior cingulate gyrus, which is the site of motivation. Anticipation of a biologically valuable consequence will motivate an animal to exhibit a particular behaviour. These limbic system functions associated with the hypothalamic innate behaviour functions are common to all vertebrates and seem to represent the id in humans.

The ego is a central component of self, and is thought to involve the neocortex, both the fourth and fifth functional systems, and associated regulatory systems. The super-ego is likely to be embodied in part of the fifth functional system and the regulatory systems attached to it. Social and cultural criteria may be generated in the parietolateral area of the association cortex, and the prefrontal area would refer to these criteria prior to interfering with the ego or id.

NEURAL CONTROL AND WILL

An important basis for interpreting the structural-functional relationships in the brain is provided by control theories. For example, reflexes are a classic control in which a reflex centre acts as a controller upon a skeletomuscular system as a control object. Compound movements involve a function generator such as a rhythm generator in addition to the classic control system structures. Mechanisms of innate behaviours are more complicated than those of compound movements and include an internal programme for complex behavioural responses. The cerebellum is connected to reflex pathways and compound movement systems, and there is some evidence suggesting the possible involvement of the cerebellum in innate behaviour.

The cerebellum as an adaptive unit enables a control to be performed in a feedforward manner without relying upon feedback (Ito, 1993). Precise performance of a feedforward control system is achieved when a controller has dynamics inversely equal to the dynamics of its control object. Therefore, the cerebellum as part of the controller is expected to represent inverse dynamics of the control object. It has recently been reported that Purkinje cell activity in the ventral paraflocculus during ocular movements elicited by movement of the whole visual field indeed represents inverse dynamics of eyeballs (Shidara, Kawano, Gomi, & Kawato, 1995). The ocular following is a reflexive movement driven by a visual signals processed in the cerebral cortex.

The role of the cerebellum in connection with the fourth and fifth functional systems in the cerebral neocortex has been interpreted as the provision of internal models in the following manner. Consider a cerebellar unit fed by input signals common to a system to be copied, and detecting discrepancies of outputs as error signals. When the error signals are fed to the cerebellar unit to induce self-reorganization of its neuronal networks, the signal transfer characteristics of the cerebellar unit will be modified to result in minimization of the error signals until the cerebellar unit becomes a model having signal transfer characteristics identical to those of the system to be copied.

I interpreted the loop connection between the motor area of the cerebral neocortex and the paravermal cortex of the cerebellum as a voluntary motor control utilizing such a model in the cerebellum (Ito, 1984). When the motor cortex sends command signals to a skeletomuscular system to perform a voluntary movement, the same signals may be sent to a model of the skeletomuscular system, the output of which is returned back to the motor cortex. Thus, a voluntary movement may be performed without using the external sensory feedback in response to the actual movement, but instead by relying upon internal feedback through a model in the cerebellum. This control system explains why movement exercise increases skill, because a cerebellar model of a skeletomuscular system is formed during the movement exercise. The control system also explains dysmetria, a typical cerebellar symptom. Whereas a healthy person can point to his or her nose accurately with a fingertip, even with closed eyes, a patient with a cerebellar disease becomes unable to do so, apparently due to lack of a cerebellar model for the finger-to-nose pointing movement.

Since the cerebellar hemisphere is connected to the cerebral cortex in parallel rather than in a loop as in the paravermis, Kawato, Furukawa, and Suzuki (1987) proposed that the cerebellum forms a model that acts as a controller to replace the motor cortex. While the motor cortex controls the performance of a voluntary movement by referring to sensory feedback, a cerebellar model is formed to replace the motor cortex as the controller. If this happens, a voluntary movement may be performed automatically by the cerebellum without conscious efforts to operate the motor cortex. These two types of model-based control may represent two stages of motor learning: first, the control is made feedforward using a cerebellar model of the skeletomuscular system, and second, it is performed unconsciously by passing the motor cortex through a cerebellar model.

These control systems for voluntary movements have been extended to explain thought processes for which the prefrontal area acts as a controller to manipulate images, concepts, or ideas generated in the parietolateral area as control objects (Ito, 1993, 1997). While the thought process is repeated, a model of images, concepts, or ideas will be formed in the cerebellum so that the thought process can be performed in a feedforward manner without feedback. If a cerebellar model replaces the prefrontal cortex, the thought process can be conducted without conscious attention.

These control systems view mental activities as a form of control, and explain mechanisms of thought by analogy with movement. In the same way as we move arms and legs, we move images, concepts, and ideas in our mind. The objects to be controlled are very different in movement and thought, but the control system principles could be identical in operation. The control system principles thus have a wide application to problems of both movement and thought (Ito, 1993, 1997).

Any control system is operated by instruction signals. In both voluntary movement and thought, the instruction signals correspond to the will that initiates these actions. Will is a positive aspect of consciousness as contrasted with the passive nature of awareness. Studies of voluntary movement and thought control lead us to problems of consciousness from this positive aspect of consciousness. The motor area receives instruction signals from the premotor and supplementary motor areas. The supplementary motor area is the source of the readiness potential that arises prior to the onset of a voluntary movement and is thought to represent a neural event underlying formation of the will to move (Deeke, Scheid, & Kornhuber, 1969). Eccles (1994) proposed that the supplementary motor area is the ultimate source of will in the brain, which interacts with the mind. However, most neuroscientists believe that neuronal activities in the supplementary motor area are driven by neuronal activities in other areas of the brain. Anatomical studies have revealed inputs to the supplementary motor area from sensory association areas and cingulate gyrus, and therefore it appears that sensory and emotional signals are integrated in the supplementary area as instruction signals for voluntary movement. However, the question as to how such an activity in the supplementary motor area gives rise to a subjective sense of will is unclear.

COMPUTATION IN THE BRAIN

The brain is an assembly of numerous neurons that interact with each other through excitatory and inhibitory synapses. Some synapses exhibit plasticity so that the signal transmission efficacy across them is activity- or experience-dependently modifiable. Hebb's (1949) classic concept is that such a neuron assembly is capable of changing its network function due to synaptic plasticity and so is capable of learning by experience. When neurons are arranged in multiple layers with synaptic plasticity incorporated in at least one layer, the neuron assembly acquires high learning capabilities, as demonstrated in the Simple Perceptron theory (Rosenblatt, 1962). As the number of layers with synaptic plasticity increases, a multilayered Perceptron model gains increased computational power (Rumelhart, Hinton, & Williams, 1986). For example, any nonlinear equation can be encoded in this type of multi-layered network by learning (Funahashi, 1989).

For the present, however, the cerebellum is the only site where both network and control theories have been successfully applied to define its adaptive mechanisms and its roles in adaptive control and internal-model-based control. The selection-stabilization mechanism of the basal ganglia seems to be based on the winner-takes-all type of network principle, but the exact mechanisms and roles of the basal ganglia have yet to be defined. Multilayered perceptrons reproduce the capabilities of the neocortex to some extent, but the back-propagation of error signals adopted in them does not seem to apply to the neocortex. An important task in neuroscientific research is to define precisely unique mechanisms and roles for all the divisions of the brain.

Even though the so-called neurocomputer based on the multilayered perceptron principles produces learning-memory capabilities, it is uncertain whether the neurocomputer can also reproduce other brain functions. Some scientists have tried to find distinct molecular mechanisms of computation, but evidence is still sparse. The occurrence of event-related potentials, such as the readiness potential mentioned earlier, suggests operation of a large neural system. The frontal mental theta wave appears in the frontal lobe when a subject tries to solve a difficult thought task (Sasaki, Tsujimoto, Nambu, Matsuzaki, & Kyuhou, 1994), suggesting that an oscillatory network operation underlies the thought process.

COMMENTS

Various ways of approaching the problems of consciousness have been discussed; however, a crucial question arises as to how we can study subjective conscious experiences such as will, affect, and self-consciousness with objective scientific methods and techniques. Once the functional localization of consciousness in the brain is identified and techniques for its objective measurement are available, consciousness will become a problem of experimental neuroscience. We shall continue our research until we localize consciousness in the brain or conclude that techniques to do this cannot be developed. A theoretical approach is to determine whether artificial consciousness can be created and realized. There has been one serious attempt achieving this (Dennett, 1997), but the results are still unclear.

REFERENCES

Crick, F., & Koch, C. (1990). Towards a neurobiological theory of consciousness. *Seminars in Neuroscience, 2,* 263–275.

Deeke, L., Scheid, P., & Kornhuber, H.H. (1969). Distribution of readiness potential, pre-motion positivity, and motor potential of the human cerebral cortex preceding voluntary finger movement. *Experimental Brain Research, 7,* 158–168.

Dennett, D.C. (1997). Consciousness in human and robot minds. In M. Ito, Y. Miyashita, & E.T. Rolls (Eds.), *Cognition, computation, and consciousness* (pp. 17–29). Oxford: Oxford University Press.

Eccles, J.C. (1994). *How the self controls its brain.* Berlin: Springer-Verlag.

Freud, S. (1923). *The ego and the id* (standard edition, 19: 12–66). London: Hogarth Press (1961).

Funahashi, K. (1989). On the approximate realisation of continuous mappings by neural networks. *Neural Networks, 2,* 183–192.

Gallup, G.G. Jr. (1985). Do minds exist in species other than our own? *Neuroscience and Biobehavioral Reviews, 9,* 631–641.

Hebb, O. (1949). *The organization of behavior.* New York: Wiley.

Ito, M. (1984). *The cerebellum and neural control.* New York: Raven Press.

Ito, M. (1993). Movement and thought: Identical control mechanisms by the cerebellum. *Trends in Neuroscience, 16,* 448–450.

Ito, M. (1997). Cerebellar microcomplexes and their possible roles in thought. In J.D. Schmahmann (Ed.), *The cerebellum and cognition* (pp. 475–487). San Diego, CA: Academic Press.

Kawato, M., Furukawa, K., & Suzuki, R. (1987). A hierarchical network model for control and learning of voluntary movement. *Biological Cybernetics, 57,* 169–185.

Roland, E.J. (1981). Somatotopical tuning of post-central gyrus during focal attention in man. A regional cerebral blood flow study. *Journal of Neurophysiology, 46,* 744–754.

Rosenblatt, F. (1962). *Principles of neurodynamics: Perception and the theory of brain mechanisms.* Washington, DC: Spartan Books.

Rumelhart, X., Hinton, G.E., & Williams, R.J. (1986). Learning representations by back propagating errors. *Nature*, *323*, 533–536.

Sasaki, K., Gemba, H., Nambu, A., & Matsuzaki, R. (1993). No-go activity in the frontal association cortex of human subjects. *Neuroscience Research*, *18*, 249–252.

Sasaki, K., Tsujimoto, T., Nambu, A., Matsuzaki, R., & Kyuhou, S. (1994). Dynamic activities of the frontal cortex in calculating and thinking. *Neuroscience Research*, *19*, 229–233.

Shidara, M., Kawano, M., Gomi, H., & Kawato, M. (1995). Inverse-dynamics encoding of eye movements by Purkinje cells in the cerebellum. *Nature*, *365*, 50–52.

Stuss, D.T., Picton, T.W., & Alexander, M.P. (in press). Consciousness, self-awareness and the frontal lobes. In S. Salloway, P. Malloy, & J. Duffy (Eds.), *The frontal lobes and neuropsychiatric illness*. Washington: American Psychiatric Press Inc.

Urade, Y., Kitahama, K., Ohishi, H., Kaneko, T., Mizuno, N., & Hayaishi, O. (1993). Dominant expression of mRNA for prostaglandin D synthase in leptomeninges, chorioid plexus, and oligodendrocytes of the adult rat brain. *Proceedings of the National Academy of Sciences USA*, *90*, 9070–9074.

Yanagihara, D., & Kondo, I. (1996). Nitric oxide plays a key role in adaptive control of locomotion in cats. *Proceedings of the National Academy of Sciences USA*, *96*, 13292–13297.

INTERNATIONAL JOURNAL OF PSYCHOLOGY, 1998, *33* (3), 199–212

EEG Aspects of Cognitive Processes: A Contribution to the Proteus-like Nature of Consciousness

Hellmuth Petsche and Susan C. Etlinger
University of Vienna, Austria

Probability mapping of amplitude and coherence based on spectral analysis yields information on the cooperation of brain areas in cognitive processes. The method is based on comparing these two parameters during the performance of a mental task with the respective values of the EEG at rest. For each of 6 frequency bands spanning the entire EEG spectrum the data are represented on schematic brain maps with significant changes of amplitude (entered at the sites of the 19 electrodes) and coherence (between all respective electrodes). These maps have proven to be largely task-specific in both group and individual studies. They are considered to objectify electrical manifestations of differential attention.

Le mapping de l'amplitude et de la cohérence basé sur l'analyse spectrale fournit de l'information sur la coopération des régions cérébrales dans les processus cognitifs. La méthode est fondée sur la comparaison de ces deux paramètres au cours d'une tâche mentale avec les valeurs respectives du EEG au repos. Pour chacune des six bandes de fréquence couvrant tout le spectre du EEG, les données sont représentées sur des cartes schématiques du cerveau avec les changements significatifs d'amplitude (à l'entrée de 19 électrodes) et de cohérence (entre les électrodes correspondantes). Ces cartes se sont montrées très spécifiques à la tâche à la fois dans des études individuelles et de groupe. Elles sont vues comme une objectivation des manifestations électriques de l'attention différentielle.

At the very beginning of the EEG era, Hans Berger (1929), who was first to record electrical signals from the intact scalp, had hoped to have found a key to the secrets of human thinking. Unfortunately, his hope came to a dead end. Berger's only success in this respect was his finding that alpha amplitude is in some way inversely related to the level of attention. Hardly any useful evidence about mental events was obtained from the electrical signals produced by the brain before the introduction of event-related potential (ERP) methods. With the increasing sophistication of computer technology, however, data on mentation were obtained even from spontaneous EEG. In the course of our studies in this field, a wealth of results in this respect have been collected, one result of which was to enrich the concept of "consciousness" to a hue somewhat different from any

observed hitherto: consciousness is about to lose its static character and to change into a pliable property of the brain depending on its specific demands at particular instants. To underline this new aspect of consciousness, which in particular resulted from EEG coherence studies, we prefer to use the term "differential attention".

Two main aspects distinguish our approach to the study of cognitive processes by means of the EEG from other current methods: one is that we make use of the ongoing (spontaneous) EEG, the other that unusually long EEG periods are employed, seldom shorter than 1 minute, so that even complex and long-lasting cognitive tasks can be investigated. In several respects our method for the examination of cognitive tasks can be compared to taking a photo with a long exposure time of the electrical events that take place in the cortex and can be recorded from the scalp. Our

Requests for reprints should be sent to Prof. Dr. H. Petsche, Währingerstr. 17, A 1090 Wien, Austria.

This research was supported by the Fonds zur Förderung der wissenschaftlichen Forschung, the Austrian Academy of Sciences, and the Gesellschaft der Musikfreunde in Wien. The authors wish to thank Mrs. Anni Schneider for experimental assistance.

experience with the two EEG parameters *amplitude (AMP)* and *coherence (COH)* in particular—obtained by spectral analysis—has revealed them as appropriate means for yielding information on the physiological processes underlying thinking.

We shall demonstrate this with some examples: listening to music, listening to a text, doing mental arithmetic, and contemplating pictures. One fundamental idea underlying our approach is the fact that mental processes are accompanied by numerous interactions between different brain areas. Some of these interactions are reflected in the EEG and can be visualized by means of the parameter coherence, which yields electrical correlations of different brain regions in terms of frequencies. There is increasing evidence that the extent of electrical correlations reflects functional cooperation (Nunez, 1995).

Our strategy can be briefly outlined as follows: in order not to miss any relevant data, the EEG is recorded from the entire scalp, as commonly occurs in hospitals, with 19 equally distributed electrodes (Jasper's 10–20 system, 1958) with respect to the averaged signals obtained from both ear lobes. After Fast Fourier Transform, averaged power and cross-power spectra are computed. For the reduction of the vast number of data, broad-band parameters are extracted for six frequency bands within the clinically relevant EEG spectrum (1.5 to 31.5Hz). For each band, AMP is computed for each electrode and COH for all 171 possible pairings of electrodes. Our procedure is based on comparing EEG periods of 1 minute or more while a certain mental task is performed with EEG periods at rest, in which free-floating thinking is allowed. In order not to succumb to the copious data, only significant differences between the data during a task and the averaged EEG at rest are considered. The method was described by Rappelsberger and Petsche in 1988. It has proven useful to map the topography of the differences of each of these two parameters on brain schemata separately for each frequency band. The resulting patterns are grids of connecting lines between brain areas, which indicate the topography of significantly increased or decreased cooperation with respect to the EEG at rest. In addition, significant changes of AMP due to the cognitive task in question are indicated by full black (for increase) or empty white (for decrease) circles at the electrode sites. To return to our earlier comparison with photography: this procedure can be compared with taking a picture with fairly long exposure time from the top of a sky-scraper in a big city at night; on such a photo the headlights of the cars leave traces, allowing one to judge in which streets the traffic is heaviest and which crossroads are most used.

Even our first experiments with this procedure surprised us by the considerable topographic variety of changes of cooperation found during cognitive tasks as compared with the EEG at rest (Petsche, Pockberger, & Rappelsberger, 1986). In order not to fall into a trap and not to attach too much importance to possibly accidental events, we first studied groups of subjects who had worked on the same cognitive tasks. Most of the findings reported in this paper are based on group experiments. Yet in order to demonstrate how the data are represented, the first sample deals with a single case study.

Figure 1 presents the findings in a 28-year-old hobby musician while he was listening, via earphones, to the first movement of a Mozart quartet for 5 minutes. The six columns of brain schemata are for the six frequency bands and represent both hemispheres and a dorsal view of the brain, for the representation of ipsilateral and interhemispheric changes of the two parameters AMP and COH with respect to the EEG at rest. The lines in these diagrams connect electrode sites between which COH has significantly increased (the full lines) or decreased (dashed lines, respectively) by listening to Mozart, as compared with the averaged EEG at rest before and after listening. The connecting lines have three different thicknesses for indicating three different P values ($P \leq .01$, $P \leq .02$, $P \leq .05$). In addition to changes of COH, significant ($P \leq .05$) AMP changes with respect to the EEG at rest are indicated by the full black (for increases) and the empty white (for decreases) circles at electrode sites.

These patterns clearly demonstrate that listening to music modifies the EEG with respect to its values at rest in this subject: changes of both AMP and COH while listening to music can be seen in several frequency bands and at different locations.

A careful description of these graphs will facilitate their interpetation. We shall begin with the *beta 2* band (18.5–31.5Hz), where most changes can be seen: the entire right hemisphere is covered by a grid of highly significant COH increases, whereas on the left hemisphere the grid is concentrated in the temporal and frontal areas. Moreover, there is increased frontal cooperation between the two hemispheres. In *beta 1* (13–18Hz), the same condition predominates but

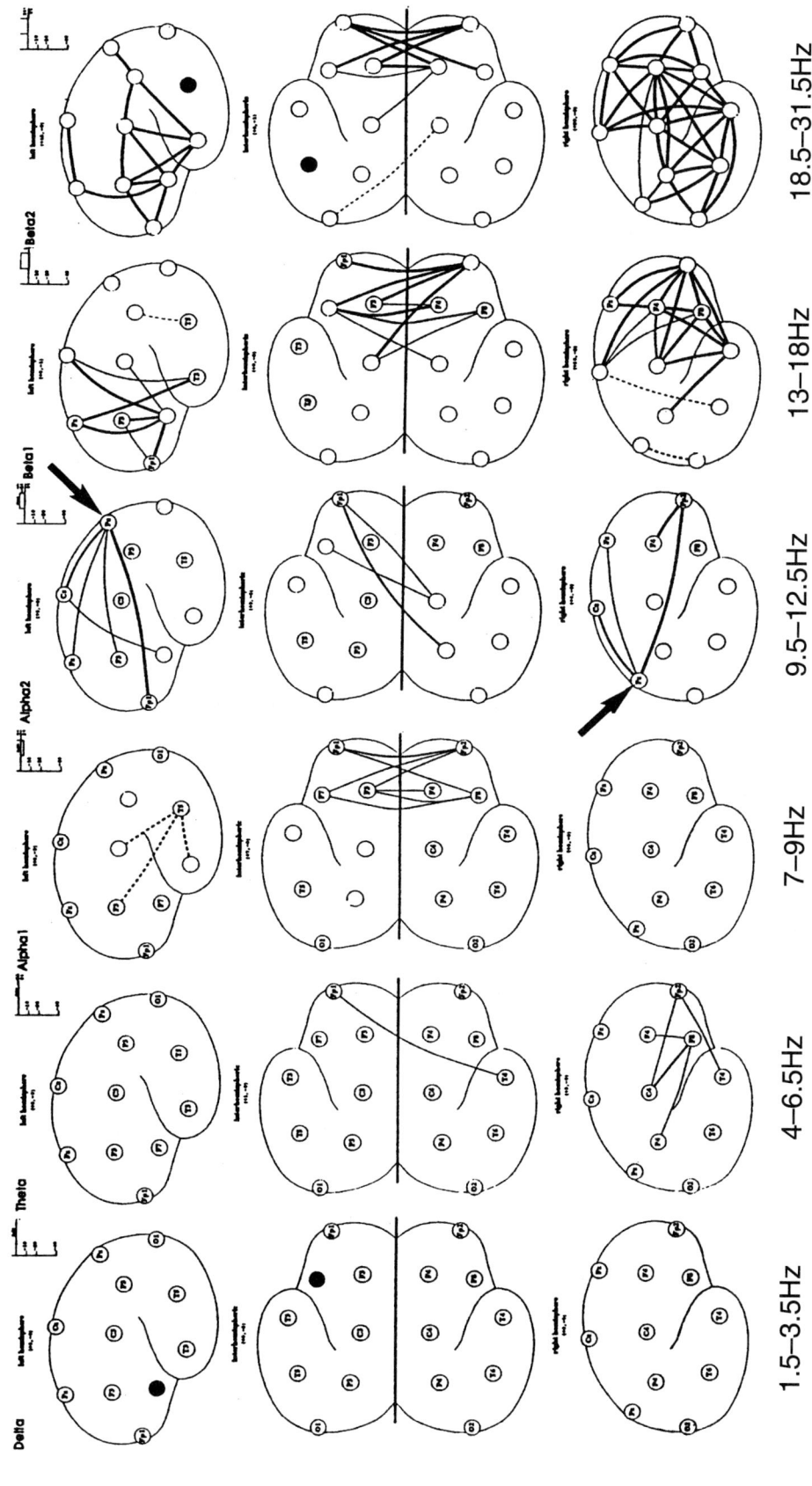

FIG. 1. (312a), a 28-year-old male, listening for 5 minutes to the first movement of Mozart quartet KV 458. Significant changes of amplitude ($P \leq .05$) and coherence ($P \leq .01, .02, .05$) with respect to EEG at rest with eyes closed.

201

is contained more frontally. In *alpha 2* (9.5–12.5Hz), the only finding worth reporting is an accumulation of coherence increases concentrated at Pz (a "nodal point", arrow) and extending out to the frontal parts of both hemispheres. *Alpha 1* (7–9Hz), on the other hand, shows increased interhemispheric cooperation only between the frontal lobes, as in the beta bands.

As for AMP, decreases are abundant in the *beta* bands and predominate on the right side. Only a few isolated sites with AMP increases are found.

While this proband is listening to music most of the changes of the two relevant parameters occured in *beta 2* and in the right hemisphere, wherein cooperation between the two frontal lobes was increased.

This pattern allows the following neurophysiological conclusions: the significant decrease of AMP at all electrode sites of the right hemisphere in *beta 2* shows that local synchronization is attenuated at these places ("event-related desynchronization", Pfurtscheller & Aranibar, 1977). This can be considered as a sign of locally increased neuronal participation in the processing of relevant data. Yet, at the same time, functional cooperation between all of these sites is significantly increased. This indicates that—with respect to the EEG at rest—for the performance of the processes involved in this cognitive task, all respective sites are heavily demanding increased cooperation of neighbouring and even of several farther distant districts of the cortex. The same is true of the frontal cooperation between the two hemispheres. We call this kind of EEG pattern, decreasing power together with increasing coherence, mode "C" processing. There is strong evidence from numerous cognitive studies performed in the same way that the occurrence of mode "C" processing at a nodal point (i.e. an electrode site that is a centre of many "spokes" of increased COH) is of primary significance for cortical data processing. Such evidence reflects processing both local, increased activities on the neuronal level (i.e. desynchronization) and increased distant (i.e. with other sites) synchronization with regard to the EEG at rest. In this example, all electrode sites of the right hemisphere are involved in mode "C" processing. In *beta 2* the most important sites in this respect are evidently F4 in the right and F7 in the left hemisphere, from whence the largest number of "spokes" emerge, thus demonstrating stronger cooperation with the same and the contralateral hemisphere. In *alpha 2* it is Pz (arrow)

from where cooperation with both frontal parts of both hemispheres and with the other two midline electrode sites is augmented.

Increasingly the evidence is accumulating that nodal points with mode "C" processing are a macro-manifestation of what Damasio postulated with his concept of "convergence zones" (1990). In his theory of "time-locked multiregional retroactivation" Damasio proposes a "recursive, iterative design to substitute for the traditional unidirectional processing cascades". One of his main arguments is that a considerable amount of integration is presumed to take place early on in the system before higher-order cortical areas are reached and that it can be reinvoked there too, without the intervention of rostral integrative structures. "Meaning is reached by the time-locked multiregional retroactivation of widespread fragment records". Three items of Damasio's hypothesis are of importance for our results and have been partly confirmed by these: (1) that the integration of multiple aspects of reality depends on the time-locked co-activation of geographically separate sites of neuronal activity; (2) that the representations of physical structure components of entities are recorded in precisely the same neural ensembles in which corresponding activity occurred during perception; and (3) that the pertinent linkages of this physical structure (their spatial and temporal coincidences) are stored in neuronal ensembles called "convergence zones", which Damasio thinks function as a sort of pivot (Damasio, Tranel, & Damasio, 1991).

It is evident that processing music is a highly individual, personality-specific event. Therefore, and in the search for possible invariant features during listening to music, we studied an unselected group of 28 males who listened to the same piece, the first movement of Mozart's D-minor string quartet (KV 458). Surprisingly, even in this large group COH changes with respect to the EEG at rest were found (Fig. 2), with characteristic features. This observation is even more meaningful, as these results represent no less than 28×5min (= 140min) of EEG recording during listening to the same piece of music; these 2hrs and 20min of EEG recording compared with EEG at rest recordings of $28 \times 2 = 56$min are compressed into the six diagrams presented in Fig. 2.

In this series, significant increases of AMP were found almost only in *delta* (1.5–3.5 Hz) bands in the right frontal area; in the remaining frequency bands AMP decreases predominated.

For COH, and starting with nodal points of mode "C", i.e. with decreasing power and increasing cortical cooperation, putative areas of primary significance for cerebral data processing—those with the largest numbers of "spokes" (marked by arrows)—are mainly found at midtemporal sites, in the right hemisphere (in more frequency bands and with more "spokes" than in the left). Once more, the upper frequency bands seem to be of particular importance for the processing of music (arrow in *beta 1*), with the exception of *delta* and *theta* with conspicuous midtemporal nodal points in the left hemisphere at T3 (arrows) and also at F7, fronto-basally, from where many connections of increased cooperation with the right hemisphere extend. This situation, however, is not specific to listening to music but is also found while listening to speech, as Fig. 3 will demonstrate. In this respect it is also worth mentioning that in this group of right-handers, mainly the left, speech-dominant hemisphere, is concerned.

An additional finding shown in Fig. 2 is worth mentioning: the frontal COH decreases between sites of decreasing AMP in the two *alpha* bands. At these sites cortico-cortical cooperation is lower than at rest and simultaneously local event-related desynchronization takes place; therefore, local increased participation in data processing of the mental task in question is enhanced. This condition, which we have called mode "D", was also often observed in other cognitive acts, particularly if creative moments are needed, suggesting that these sites may be involved, in this frequency band, in cortico-subcortical instead of cortico-cortical exchange of data (i.e. with the dorso-median thalamus probably becoming coactivated). This in turn lends itself to the assumption that this frontal and mainly frontopolar decrease of AMP is caused by an activation of those large groups of prefrontal cells that were found (Fuster, 1989) to discharge in his delayed response experiments and which Fuster interprets as a manifestation of short-term memory.

As for the many interhemispheric coherence increases in *theta* and *delta*, most of which seem to traverse the brain in oblique directions, they suggest that subcortical structures, most likely the thalamus, may be involved. Cortico-cortical bundles of fibres cannot mediate these COH increases, because callosal fibres almost exclusively connect symmetric sites of the cortex.

Figure 3 shows the results of another group study, in which 17 males were requested to listen to a newspaper text for 5min with their eyes closed. So, these diagrams represent in sum 1hr 25 min of EEG recording during a single task. Contrary to the findings while listening to music, listening to a text causes AMP increases at many sites, mainly in the *delta* and *beta* bands; no decreases of AMP were found. Obviously AMP changes with regard to the EEG at rest were not strong enough to show up significantly.

Also the patterns of COH changes differ greatly from those during music: while listening to text, maximum nodal points occurred mainly in *theta* in the left mid-temporal and fronto-basal areas (arrows), but also temporo-occipitally on the right side (arrow). No nodal points appeared in *alpha* and *beta* on the right side, contrary to the situation when listening to music. In this context it may be worth mentioning that nodal points at F7 were also found in experiments with simultaneous interpreters when they were required to "shadow" texts (i.e. mentally repeat the texts). So an activation of Broca's area may underlie this phenomenon.

These findings may briefly be summarized as follows: the EEG during listening to Mozart differed from listening to speech mainly by the emergence of nodal points of mode "C" (increased COH and decreased AMP; i.e. "event-related *de*synchronization" according to Pfurtscheller & Aranibar, 1977) in both midtemporal areas, in the right more than in the left hemisphere, and in almost all frequency bands, whereas, while listening to speech, almost only left temporal nodal points were found, and these exclusively in the lower frequency bands. In addition, for music, event-related desynchronization was found in numerous frequency bands and all over the cortex, but none at all was observed while listening to the newspaper text. All these findings support the assumption that listening to music challenges the cortex more and in more regions of both hemispheres than listening to a newspaper text.

The sites with increases of both AMP and COH (mode "A" processing) deserve additional discussion. At such sites both local and distant synchronization are higher than at rest. In our view, such regions, even if obviously significantly involved in processing the cognitive task in question, do this secondarily as compared with sites of mode "C" processing. Their task may be more auxiliary than the latter (Pfurtscheller, Stancak, & Neuper, 1996, call this phenomenon "event-related synchronization").

Needless to say, these findings were tested for specificity in different ways; group experiments,

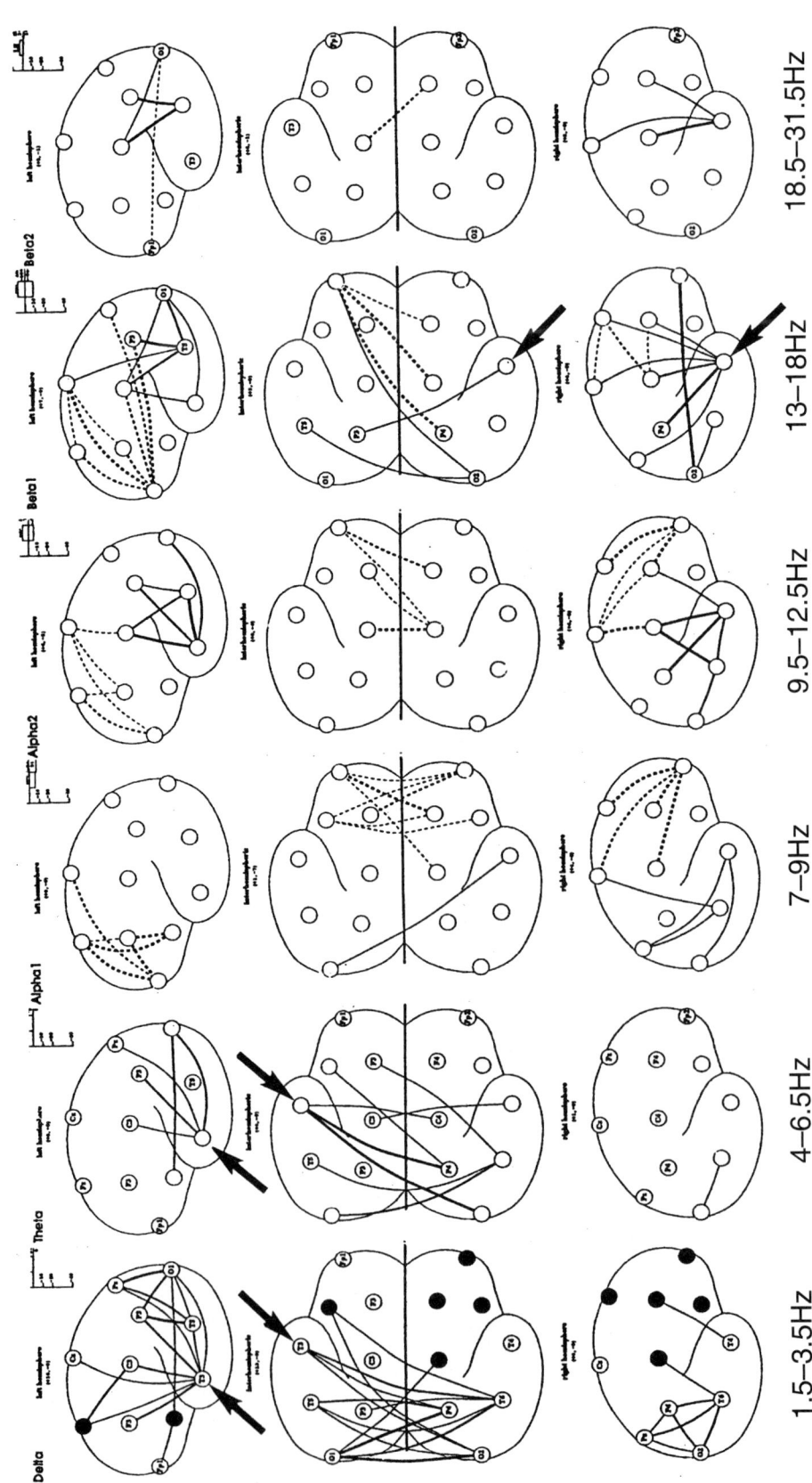

FIG. 2. Twenty-eight males listening to the same piece as in Fig. 1. Significant changes of amplitude ($P \leq .05$) and coherence ($P \leq .01, .02, .05$) with respect to EEG at rest with eyes closed.

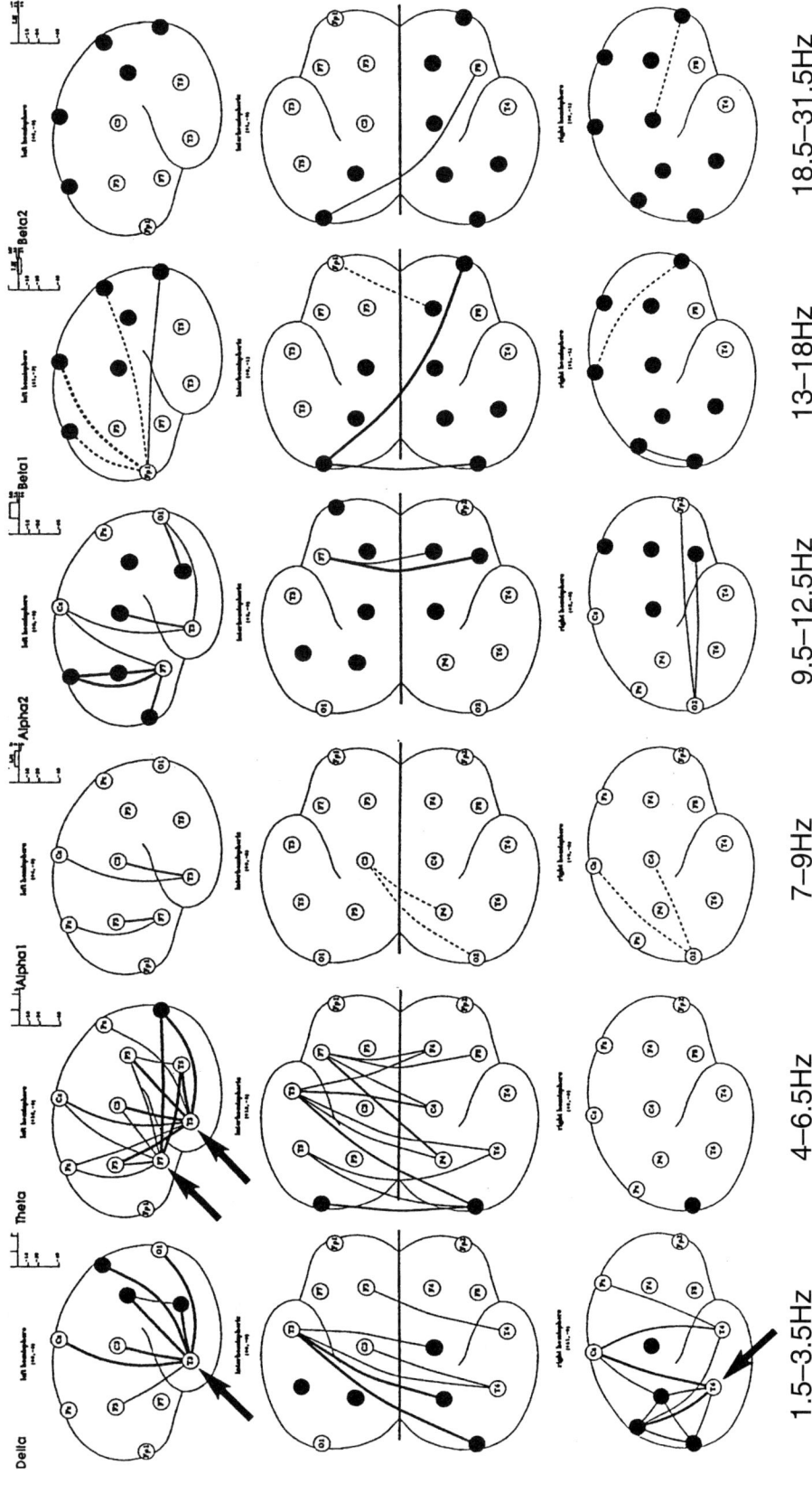

FIG. 3. Seventeen subjects (8 males, 9 females) listening to a text. Significant changes of amplitude ($P \leq .05$) and coherence ($P \leq .01, .02, .05$) with respect to EEG at rest with eyes closed.

205

in which the same tasks were repeated after 6 and 12 weeks, brought surprising concurrences. Moreover, music from different composers would produce different COH patterns (Petsche, Richter, Von Stein, Etlinger, & Filz, 1993).

The following examples concern other categories of thinking. One is mental arithmetic (Fig. 4). In this study, 16 subjects, half of them females, were requested to add subsequent numbers mentally, beginning with 1, and to tell the result after 1min of calculating. The figure shows the averaged significant changes of the two EEG parameters observed under this task with respect to the EEG at rest with eyes closed. Compared to the previous tasks, mental arithmetic produced more COH changes in *delta* and *theta*, with mode "C" processing predominating in *theta*, the sensory regions of the brain being most involved by this task (arrows indicate the maximum nodal points). It is also worth mentioning that, in the upper frequency bands, more processing seems to go on in the left than in the right hemisphere. This may be due to the chiefly logical character of mental arithmetic operations. However, the strong midtemporal involvement in *alpha 2* and *beta 1* could be an indication that silent speaking while calculating could be implied. Just as while listening to Mozart, this task also induced many frontopolar COH decreases in the upper frequency bands, beginning with *alpha 1*.

The unusually large number of COH increases in *delta* and also *theta* deserves special mention and may be due to the special demands on working memory by this task.

A final example concerns visual thinking (Fig. 5). Together with Kaplan (1995), we studied 38 females who were requested to contemplate 4 separate slides, each presenting one painting from different periods in the history of the Fine Arts, and to try to keep them in memory. Each of these pictures was presented for 2min. Thus, these diagrams represent a period of time of $4 \times 2 \times 38$min or 5hrs and 4min of EEG recording time for these tasks. Again, the averaged EEGs were compared with the averaged EEGs at rest, but this time with eyes opened.

It is no surprise that such an extremely complex visual task gives rise to a large number of significant AMP and COH changes in all frequency bands with respect to the averaged EEG at rest. Discussing them in detail would go beyond the scope of this paper. Therefore, only a few especially salient features will be mentioned. One most striking finding is the large number of COH decreases emerging from occipital and parietal regions in the lower frequency bands (Fig. 5a, arrows). This means that these regions *reduced* their cooperation with other cortical areas while the pictures were being contemplated. (In contrast to this, cortico-cortical cooperation with many mode "C" sites increased in the same areas in the *beta* bands.) Contemplating a picture demands an extensive exchange of information between the occipital cortex and subcortical sites, mainly the lateral geniculate. It could be that this increased cooperation with subcortical regions takes place at the expense of cortico-cortical cooperation, which therefore was reduced with respect to the EEG at rest. The lower frequency bands seem to be particularly engaged in this process. Simultaneously with the diminutions in COH, AMP was reduced at many sites, mainly in *alpha* and *beta*, yet increased in *delta* and *theta*, indicating partly primary, partly secondary cerebral data processing, respectively.

The assumption of increased cortico-subcortical cooperation while contemplating the pictures is supported by the following findings: the same group was requested to memorize, as vividly as possible, the same pictures as seen earlier (Fig. 5b). The two tasks, contemplating and memorizing, were separated by 1min of silent reading, for distraction.

In the case of memorizing the same four pictures, for 2min each (Fig. 5b), occipital COH decreases are almost completely absent, replaced by a large number of increased cortico-cortical interactions. Besides, many of the sites in the lowest two frequency bands where AMP was increased while contemplating show AMP decreases while memorizing. In this task, visual input from the periphery is lacking and the cortex has become autonomously active, which also manifests itself in the increased number of nodal points of mode "C" in *theta*, suggesting increased cortico-cortical cooperation focused on occipital participation (arrows).

Another major difference between the probability patterns of these two visual tasks is the numerous COH decreases with frontopolar maxima on both sides in the *alpha* bands and *beta 1* during contemplating (Fig. 5a). In this context it should be noted that the subjects were requested to keep as many items of the pictures as possible in their memories while contemplating them. This

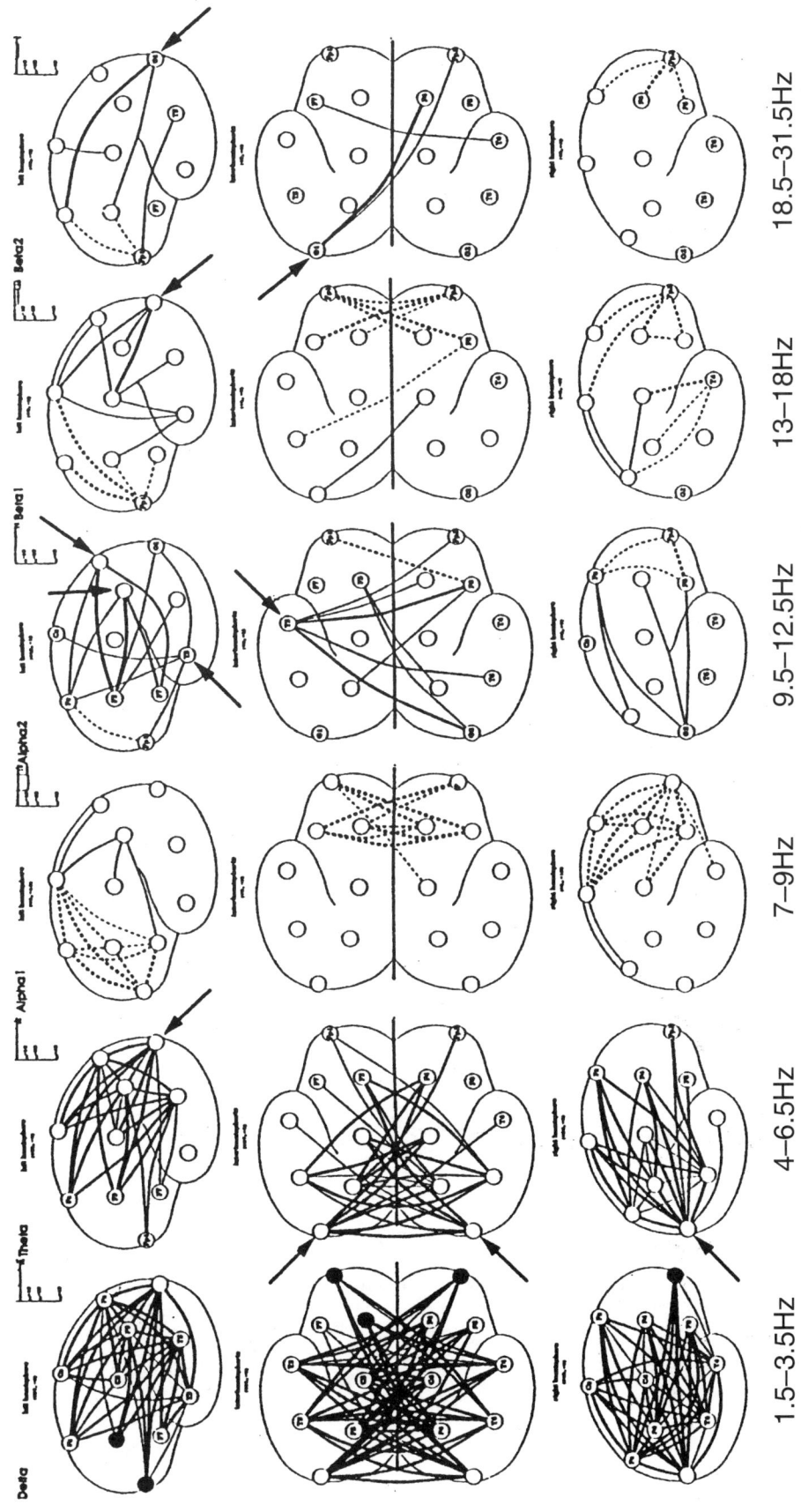

FIG. 4. Eighteen subjects (9 males, 9 females) doing mental arithmetic for 1 minute. Significant changes of amplitude ($P \le .05$) and coherence ($P \le .01, .02, .05$) with respect to EEG at rest with eyes closed.

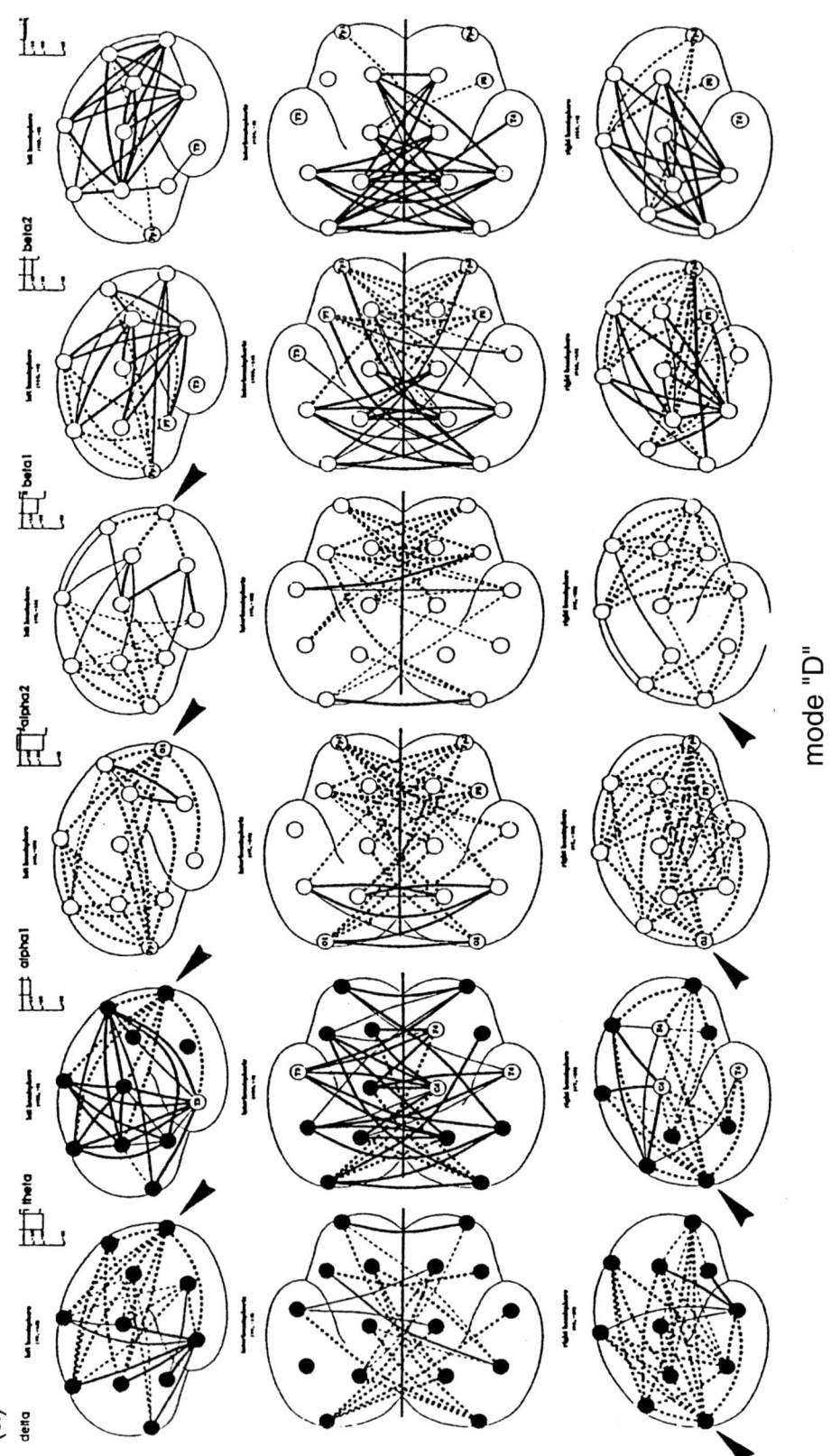

mode "D"

208

(b)

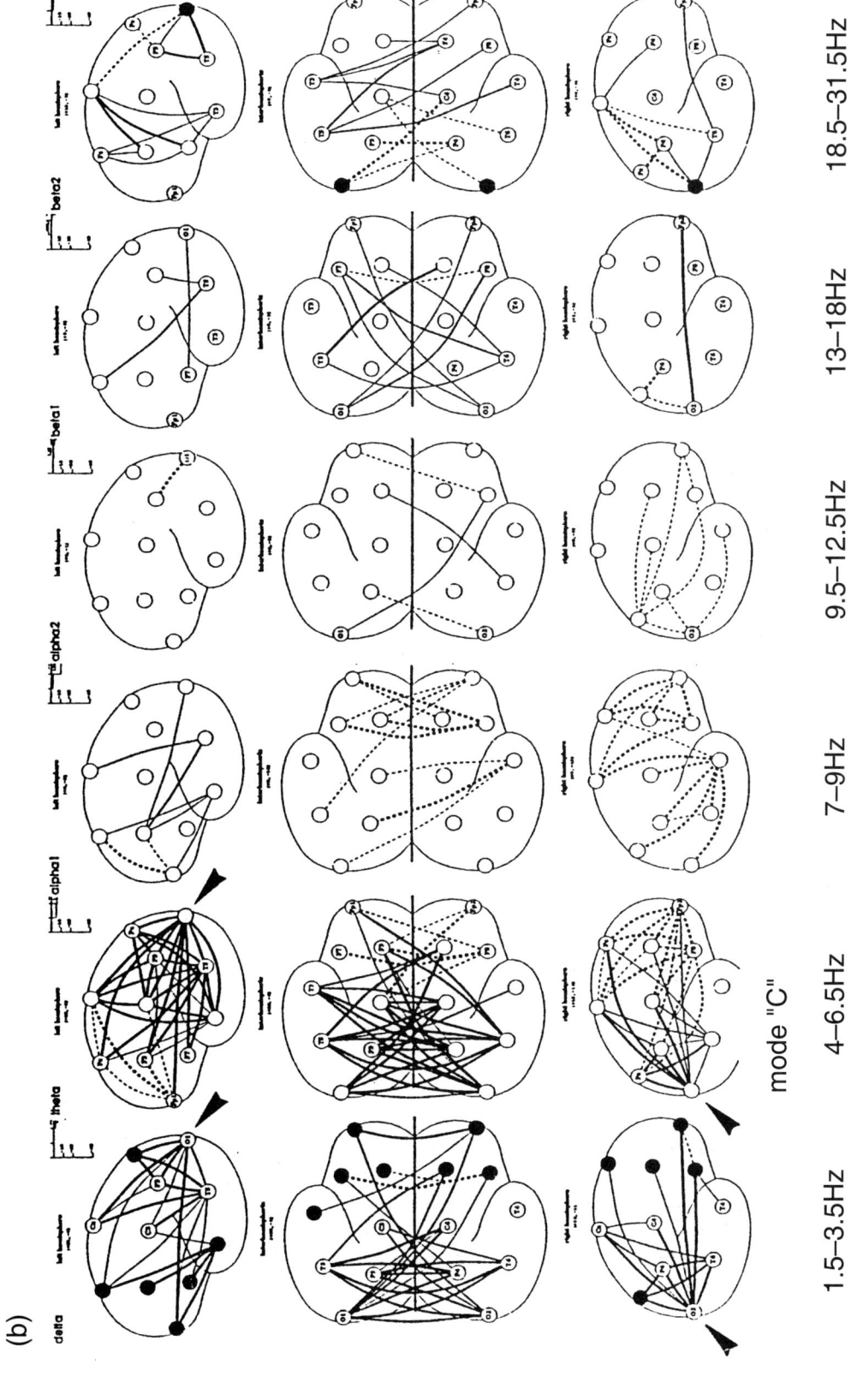

FIG. 5. (a) Thirty-eight females contemplating four pictures for 2 minutes each; (b) the same group memorizing these four pictures for 2 minutes each. Significant changes of amplitude ($P \leqslant .05$) and coherence ($P \leqslant .01, .02, .05$) with respect to EEG at rest with eyes closed.

209

abundance of frontopolar COH decreases supports the assumption, discussed earlier, that these signs of more parcellated but (with respect to at rest) increased local (neuronal) activities in the fronto-polar cortex may be interpreted as increased involvement of working memory. On the other hand, while retrieving from memory, as in Fig. 5b, fronto-topolar COH decreases were reduced in number and became evident only in *alpha 1* and *theta*.

The role of the lowest two frequency bands for storing in memory becomes manifest in the increases of AMP, which is much more pronounced in contemplating than in memorizing (in this case, "memorizing" refers to "retrieving from memory").

Comparisons of these results with those of additional tasks performed by this group, such as silent reading and mentally creating pictures, supplied further bridges to a neurophysiological interpretation of the findings.

This series provides another opportunity for the demonstration of the efficiency of this approach because the 36 subjects of this series were chosen in such a way that half of them were graduates from the Viennese Academy of Fine Arts; the others were artistically "naive". We thus felt a certain responsibility to examine whether or not EEG differences could also be found in the way the artists and the non-artists among these 38 subjects would process these pictures. Some of the results in this respect are shown in Fig. 6, where a few of the most striking differences between artists and non-artists while performing visual tasks are shown. While contemplating all pictures artists engaged their left hemisphere more than non-artists in *beta 2*, and the cooperation within the left hemisphere and between left temporal, parietal, and occipital regions and the right hemisphere was more intensive than in non-artists. In addition, the right fronto-basal and frontopolar regions of non-artists worked more autonomously while contemplating.

When asked to create an image of their own mentally, to be sketched after the EEG examination, non-artists evidently struggled more with this task than did accomplished artists in *delta*. But a conspicuous difference between both groups was also seen in the frontopolar COH decreases, in particular in *alpha* and *theta*, which were only found in artists and never in non-artists (not illustrated).

While memorizing (Fig. 6), the most striking difference was also found in the *delta* band, where artists showed more left-sided ipsilateral and also contralateral occipito-frontal cooperation than non-artists.

This is only a minute selection of our findings in order to attempt, in the future, to use the EEG for the study and assessent of artistic abilities. As for music, such differences in the EEG between musically educated and non-educated subjects have been found in group studies (Johnson, Petsche, Richter, von Stein, & Filz, 1966), and the EEG has been applied to individuals for the study of musical thinking (Holländer, Petsche, Dimitrov, Filz, & Wenger, 1997).

Instead of presenting further examples, some possible interpretations of these findings are to be discussed. Both parameters, AMP as well as COH, reflect synchronization of electric brain events, whatever this may mean. Local AMP is a hint of the amount of local synchronization in the respective frequency band, and COH hints at the degree of distant synchronization between two signals. For a signal to be recorded from the scalp, an area of at least several cm^2 of synchronized cortical activity is required (Cooper, Winter, Crow, & Walter, 1965). The estimated amount of synchronization has long been a main determinator for EEG diagnostics of brain diseases. However, such high levels of synchronization as those that underlie clinical EEG patterns in brain disturbances are far beyond the low levels of synchronization produced by cognitive processes. In contrast to the dimension of "macrosynchronization", which is seen by the naked eye and was therefore destined to become the principal pillar of clinical electroencephalography, "microsynchronization", which could not be detected before the computer-era of the EEG, turns out to reflect phenomena of mentation.

One last but principal question concerns the possible neuronal mechanisms underlying these phenomena. There is increasing evidence that the tendency of neuronal assemblies rather than of single cells to discharge synchronously is at the base of information processing by neurons (see the review by Singer, 1993). General agreement also exists in that tangential intracortical connections seem to be the substrate of synchronization, a process that may serve perceptual binding; by this term the recognition of the totality of sensory events as a conceptual entity should be understood. Moreover, perception is known today to be an exceedingly parcelled process that depends on activities distributed over a large range of geographically distinct brain regions (Edelman, 1989). These have to be concurrently activated for the recognition and understanding of events in the environment, as has also been confirmed by clinical observations (Damasio et al.,

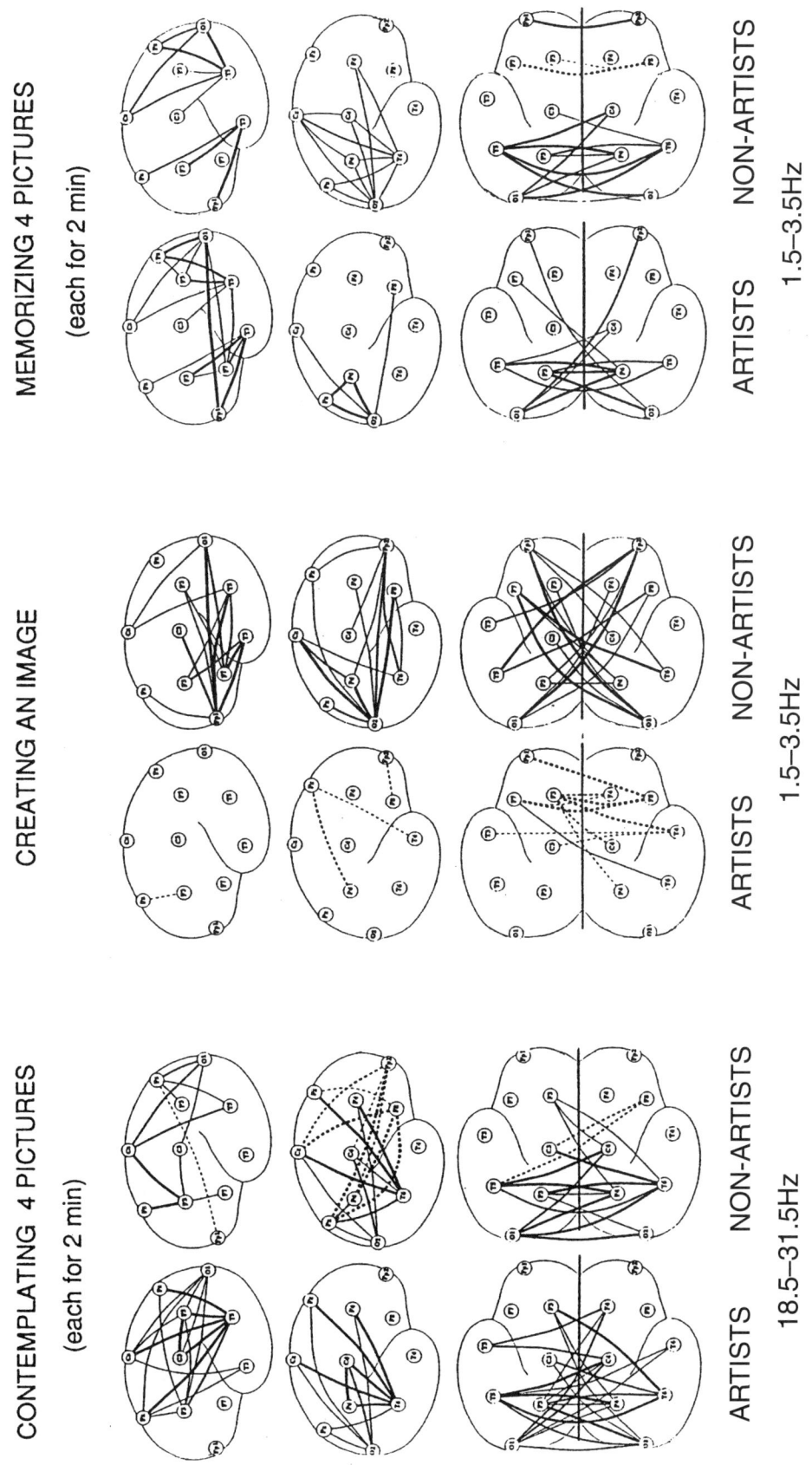

FIG. 6. Differences between artists and non-artists among the 38 subjects of Fig. 5 while contemplating and memorizing the pictures of Fig. 1 and while mentally creating a picture. Significant changes of amplitude ($P \leq .05$) and coherence ($P \leq .01, .02, .05$) with respect to EEG at rest with eyes closed.

1991). From a neuroanatomical point of view, these statements are supported by studies of Goldman-Rakic and Friedman (1991) showing that parallel-distributed cortical networks are the basis of cortical connectivity. On the micro-level, support for our way of interpreting our results is provided by the morphological studies of Braitenberg and Schüz (1991), according to which the predominant part of the neocortex is a network of mostly random connections in which convergence and divergence seem to play equally important roles.

Based on these studies, we consider the EEG to be a host of cooperative processes reflecting, in a very indirect way, cellular events in the recurrent cooperative networks of the cortex, as Abeles (1991) calls them, which have the ability to produce cooperative processes out of nerve cell discharges in large neuronal assemblies with convergent/divergent interactions.

A last word should be said about what we think of the possible functional significance of these findings with respect to consciousness: we consider them to be an electrophysiological correlate of differential attention. By this term we understand those functional states of the cortex that are needed to adjust the cortex in an optimum way to the instantaneously changing conditions induced by the environment. The electrical aspects of the topographic mosaic of differential attention, averaged over minutes, seem to manifest themselves in the continuously changing landscape of microsynchronization, reflected by the patterns of power and coherence changes concurrent with a mental task. These electric mosaics have proved to be highly task-specific and, in spite of individual variations, provide amazingly consistent interindividual EEG features even during sophisticated mental tasks.

REFERENCES

Abeles, M. (1991). *Corticonics—Neural circuits of the cerebral cortex*. Cambridge: Cambridge University Press.

Berger, H. (1929). Über das Elektrenkephalogramm des Menschen. Erste Mitteilung. *Archiv für Psychiatrie und Nervenkrankheiten, 87*, 527–570.

Braitenberg, V., & Schüz, A. (1991). *Anatomy of the cortex. Statistics and geometry*. Berlin: Springer.

Cooper, R., Winter, A.L., Crow, H.J., & Walter, W.G. (1965). Comparison of subcortical, cortical and scalp activity using indwelling electrodes in man. *Electroencephalography and Clinical Neurophysiology, 18*, 217–228.

Damasio, A.R. (1990). Synchronous activation in multiple cortical regions: A mechanism for recall. *Seminar in Neurosciences., 2*, 287–296.

Damasio, A.R., Tranel, D., & Damasio, H.C. (1991). Somatic markers and the guidance of behavior: Theory and preliminary testing. In H.S. Levin, H.M. Eisenberg, & A.L. Benton (Eds.), *Frontal lobe function and dysfunction* (pp. 217–229). New York: Oxford University Press.

Edelman, G.M. (1989). *The remembered present. A biological theory of consciousness*. New York: Basic Books.

Fuster, J.M. (1989). *The prefrontal cortex* (2nd edn.). New York: Raven Press.

Goldman-Rakic, P.S., & Friedman, H.R. (1991). The circuitry of working memory revealed by anatomy and metabolic imaging. In H.S. Levin, H. Eisenberg, & A.L. Benton (Eds.), *Frontal lobe function and dysfunction* (pp. 72–91). New York: Oxford University Press.

Holländer, I., Petsche, H., Dimitrov, L.I., Filz, O., & Wenger, E. (1997). The reflection of cognitive tasks in EEG and MRI and a method of its visualization. *Brain Topography, 9*, 177–190.

Jasper, H.H. (1958). Report of the committee on methods of clinical examination in electroencephalography. *Electroencephalography and Clinical Neurophysiology, 10*, 371–375.

Johnson, J.K., Petsche, H., Richter, P., Stein, A. von, & Filz, O. (1996). The dependence of coherence estimates of spontaneous EEG on gender and music training. *Music Perception, 13*, 563–582.

Kaplan, S. (1995). *Malerinnen—Visuelles Wahrnehmen und bildliches Vorstellen, zwezwei Aspekte einer komplexen Begabung. Eine EEG-Amplituden- und Kohärenzstudie*. Thesis, University of Vienna. Wien.

Nunez, P.L. (1995). *Neocortical dynamics and human EEG rhythms*. New York: Oxford University Press.

Petsche, H. (1996). Approaches to verbal, visual and musical creativity by EEG coherence analysis. *International Journal of Psychophysiology, 24*, 145–160.

Petsche, H., Lindner, K., Rappelsberger, P., & Gruber, G. (1988). The EEG: An adequate method to concretise brain processes elicited by music. *Music Perception, 6*, 133–159.

Petsche, H., Pockberger, H., & Rappelsberger, P. (1986). EEG topography and mental performance. In F.H. Duffy (Ed.), *Topographic mapping of the brain* (pp. 63–98). Stoneham, UK: Butterworth.

Petsche, H., Richter, P., Von Stein, A., Etlinger, S., & Filz, O. (1993). EEG coherence and musical thinking. *Music Perception, 11*, 117–151.

Pfurtscheller, G., & Aranibar, A. (1977). Event-related cortical desynchronization detected by power measurements of scalp EEG. *Electroencephalography and Clinical Neurophysiology, 42*, 817–826.

Pfurtscheller, G., Stancak, A. Jr., & Neuper, Ch. (1996). Event-related synchronization (ERS) in the alpha band—an electrophysiological correlate of cortical idling: A review. *International Journal of Psychophysiology, 24*, 39–46.

Rappelsberger, P., & Petsche, H. (1988). Probability mapping: Power and coherence analyses of cognitive processes. *Brain Topography, 1*, 46–54.

Singer, W. (1993). Synchronization of cortical activity and its putative role in information processing and learning. *Annual Reviews in Physiology, 55*, 349–374.

INTERNATIONAL JOURNAL OF PSYCHOLOGY, 1998, *33* (3), 213–225

Thoughts on the Meaning of Brain Electrical Activity

Karl H. Pribram

Stanford University and Radford University, Virginia, USA

Recordings of electrical brain activity have provided a rich field of data. These data are harvested at at least two scales of inquiry: scalp recordings from humans have accessed cognitive aspects of the mind/brain relationship, and microelectrode recordings in animals have delineated circuits involved in sensory and motor processes. As yet, there are few studies that have attempted to reconcile the findings obtained at these different scales. It is such reconciliation that we are attempting in experiments performed in our Center for Brain Research and Informational Sciences. A progress report follows.

L'enregistrement de l'activité du cerveau a fourni des données très riches qui ont alimenté au moins deux niveaux de recherche. Les enregistrements de surface chez l'humain ont permis d'étudier les aspects cognitifs de la relation esprit/cerveau tandis que les enregistrements par microélectrodes chez les animaux ont délimité les circuits sous-jacents aux processus sensoriels et moteurs. Jusqu'à maintenant, il y a eu peu d'études qui tenté de réconcilier les données obtenues à ces deux niveaux. C'est objectif que visent nos expériences au Center for Brain Research and Informational Sciences. Cet article présente un rapport d'étape.

THE ELECTROENCEPHALOGRAM

We recently completed an experiment which showed that electrical activity recorded from the scalp of humans changes its configuration on average 100 times per second. We initially recorded and displayed, on a videotape, the squared amplitude of the brain electrical activity and noted that the encoded colour representation changed much more rapidly than we expected from the years of watching the running EEG on paper or on an oscilloscope screen. (The video was shown at the conference.) In order to quantify our observation we developed a scalar representation based on drawing a line that connected the location of maximum squared amplitude during a 5msec period with the location of the maximum squared amplitude recorded during the following 5msec period. We surveyed 19 locations (in the standard 10–20 electrocap configuration) over a 30sec epoch. As the maximum amplitude moved repeatedly between the same two locations, the line between those locations became thicker. The stability of the patterns of scalars over different epochs is shown in Fig. 1.

Note that the rate of change of the electrical brain activity varies from approximately 68 to 168 per second but that the scalar patterns are practically identical whether the recording epoch is 5.5 or 20sec. The patterns do change, however, when the person engages in a mental task, as can be seen in Fig. 2. These observations suggest an answer to a persisting problem in relating brain function to psychological processes, a problem enunciated clearly by Karl Lashley (1942, p. 306):

Requests for reprints should be addressed to Karl H. Pribram, Center for Brain Research and Informational Sciences, Radford University, Box 6977, Radford, VA24142, USA (E-mail: kpribram@runet.edu).

The author is Professor Emeritus at Stanford University and James P. and Anna King University Professor and Eminent Scholar, Commonwealth of Virginia.

My thanks go to Basil Hiley and Kunio Yasue as well as to Ilya Prigogine for help in interpreting the mathematics presented here. Any remaining errors are not their responsibility—they are due to my remaining stuck in a highly dense spectral domain.

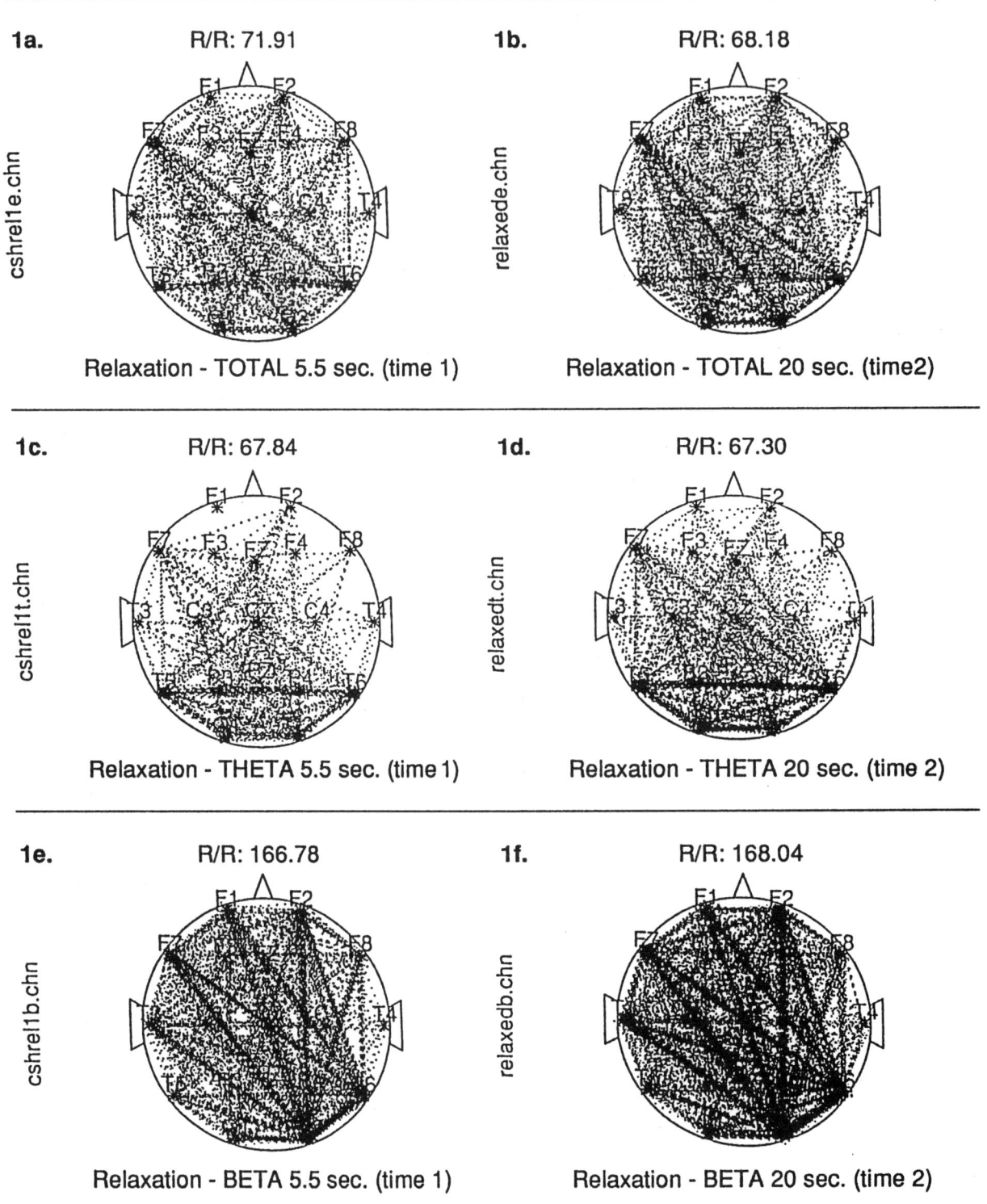

FIG. 1. Scalar representation of two different portions (early and late) and two data set lengths (5.5 and 10.0sec) of the baseline condition: Fig. 1a and 1b, total; 1c and 1d, theta; and 1e and 1f, beta.

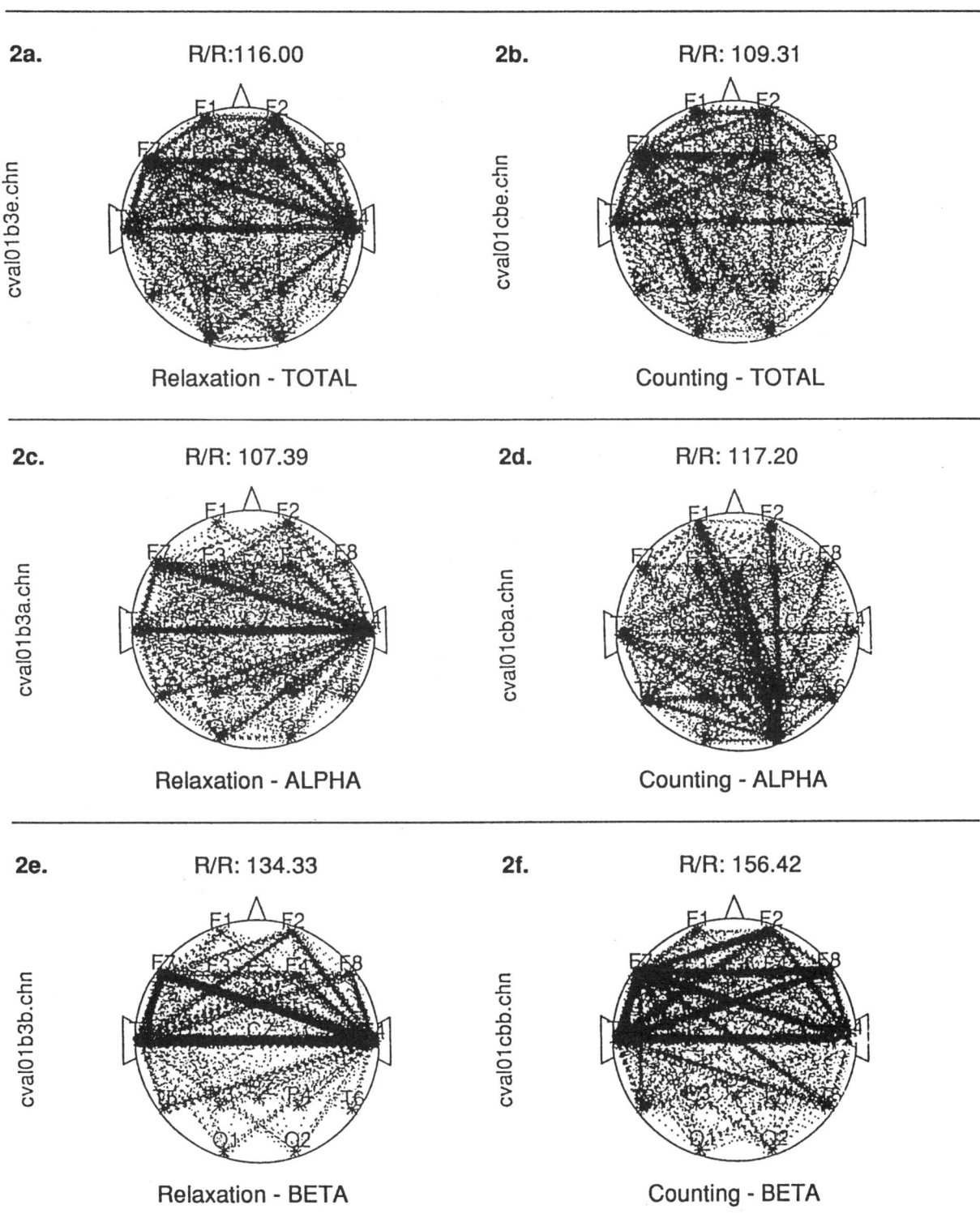

2a. R/R:116.00

cval01b3e.chn

Relaxation - TOTAL

2b. R/R: 109.31

cval01cbe.chn

Counting - TOTAL

2c. R/R: 107.39

cval01b3a.chn

Relaxation - ALPHA

2d. R/R: 117.20

cval01cba.chn

Counting - ALPHA

2e. R/R: 134.33

cval01b3b.chn

Relaxation - BETA

2f. R/R: 156.42

cval01cbb.chn

Counting - BETA

FIG. 2(a–f).   Scalar representations of recrudescence in total, alpha, and beta EEG during resting and counting backwards.

Here is the dilemma. Nerve impulses are transmitted over definite, restricted paths in the sensory and motor nerves and in the central nervous system from cell to cell through definite intercellular connections. Yet all behavior seems to be determined by masses of excitation, by the form or relations or proportions of excitation within general fields of activity, without regard to particular nerve cells. It is the pattern and not the element that counts. What sort of nervous organization might be capable of responding to a pattern of excitation without limited specialized paths of conduction? The problem is almost universal in the activities of the nervous system and some hypothesis is needed to direct further research.

For almost half a century we have known that the EEG recorded from the scalp does not so much reflect an accumulation of nerve impulses as it reflects the graded polarizations (hyper- and depolarizations) of synapses and the fine-fibred axonic and dendritic cortical connection web (e.g. Adey, 1967; Creutzfeld, 1961; Green, Maxwell, & Petsche, 1961; Green & Petsche, 1961; Li, Cullen, & Jasper, 1956; Verzeano & Laufer, 1970; Verzeano & Negishi, 1960)[1]. It is in these graded polarizations that patterns of excitations (and inhibition) need to be sought.

GRADED POLARIZATIONS IN THE BRAIN'S CONNECTION WEB

However, it is nerve impulses that we can readily record with microelectrodes, nerve impulses that are generated in order to inform one part of the nervous system what is going on in another part. This has given rise to viewing the functions of the brain and especially those of the cerebral cortex in terms of its circuitry. Though circuitry is certainly an important aspect of brain function, by themselves circuits cannot account for the psychological processes emphasized by Lashley in the earlier quotation.

As a metaphor, the old vacuum tube serves admirably. The tube's circuitry has interposed within it a plate. Minute changes in the charge of the plate provide patterns in an otherwise stable transmission of energy. These patterns, these

designs, constitute the information processing capabilities of early computers.

George Bishop (1956), in a definitive essay that discussed "the natural history of the nerve impulse", reviewed the evidence for attending another aspect of neural activity, an aspect analogous to that served by the plate in the vacuum tube. Bishop indicated that graded slow potentials, hyper- and depolarizations, are more general as well as more primitive than the impulses that probably developed when the early metazoans became too large. He cites the evidence that the cerebral cortex still operates largely by means of connections characteristic of primitive neuropil, the most appropriate mechanism for the production of a state, as contrasted to the transmission about such states. On the basis of such evidence, I suggested (Pribram, 1971, p. 105) that:

> Nerve impulses and graded potentials are two kinds of processes that can function reciprocally. A simple hypothesis would state that the less efficient the processing of synaptic arrival patterns into axonic departure patterns, the longer the duration of the designs of the graded dendritic microprocess.—In short, nerve impulses arriving at synapses generate a graded potential dendritic microprocess. The design of this microprocess interacts with that already present by virtue of the spontaneous activity of the nervous system and its previous 'experience.' The interaction is modulated by inhibitory process and the whole procedure produces effects akin to the interference patterns resulting from the interaction of simultaneously occurring wave fronts. The graded potential processes thus act as cross correlation devices to produce new figures from which the patterns of departure of nerve impulses are initiated. The rapidly paced changes in awareness could well reflect the duration of the correlation process.

One way of portraying the two different modes of operation of the brain cortex is to record, from the same microelectrode, with low and with high pass amplification. We find (Fig. 3) that the slow graded activity recorded with low pass filtering precedes the high pass filtered spiking recorded from the same electrode 75% of the time during sensory stimulation (in 2369 recordings). This indicates that, just as for intracellular recordings from axons, that depolarizations and hyperpolarizations precede the generation of action potentials (spikes). Thus, as in the case of the vacuum tube plate, the graded activity "programmes" the

---

[1] The situation is much the same as it is with the electroretinogram, where the alpha and beta waves reflect retinal activity that is entirely devoid of nerve impulses.

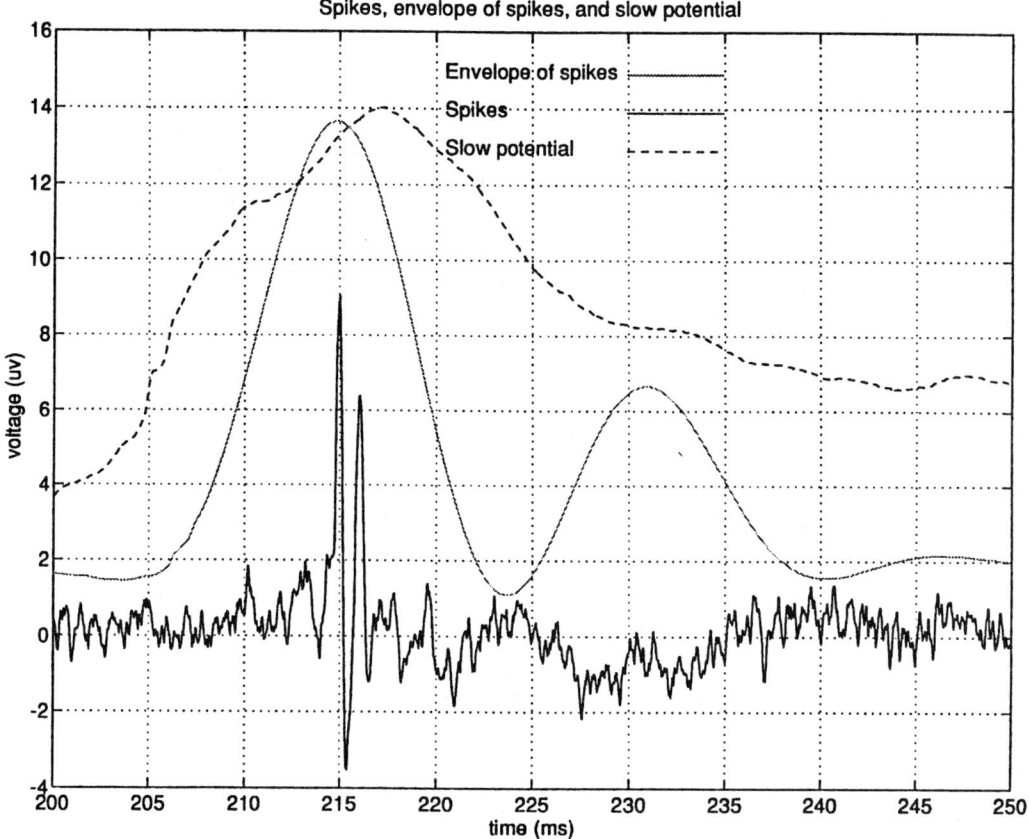

FIG. 3. An example of the relationship between spikes and multi-unit bursts to coincident local field potentials. Note that the ascending slope of the field potentials precedes that of the spikes and bursts. If the field potentials were a consequence of the burst, the peak should coincide with or come later than the maximum number of bursts.

output of the axon from which recordings are made. The graded activity intervenes between the input and the output relation of the neuron.

The evidence available at that time, albeit indirect, was reviewed to support the hypothesis that the graded processes recorded with low pass filtering, presumably occurring in dendrites, are coordinated with awareness. This evidence did not, however, include the displays of designs of dendritic processes that are the critical underpinnings of the hypothesis.

THE CONFIGURATION OF DENDRITIC FIELDS: A SPECTRAL DOMAIN

Such displays are readily provided, thanks to Kuffler (1953), who devised a technique that maps the configuration of dendritic activity from microelectrode recordings of nerve impulses from the axons connected to those dendrites. Kuffler applied to microelectrode recordings from the optic nerve the clinical technique of mapping

the visual field of a subject. Instead of obtaining a verbal or instrumental response from the subject, Kuffler obtained the response from a single axon: A dramatic increase (or decrease) from baseline spontaneous activity in the number of nerve impulses. The visual field of that axon is described by the area in the visual environment over which a stimulus is registered by the response of the axon. David Hubel, in a lecture at Stanford University, pointed out that such a visual "receptive" field actually represents the functional dendritic field of that axon under the conditions of visual stimulation.

During the 1960s and 1970s many laboratories, including mine, mapped these functional dendritic fields in the visual system. Their shapes change from concentric (bull's eye) to elongated as one proceeds from optic nerve to cortex. Mathematical descriptions and computer simulations can be fitted to these shapes (for review see, for instance Pribram, 1991, Lectures 1, 2, 4, 5). Here I present similar shapes obtained from recordings made from axons in the somatosensory cortex of rats

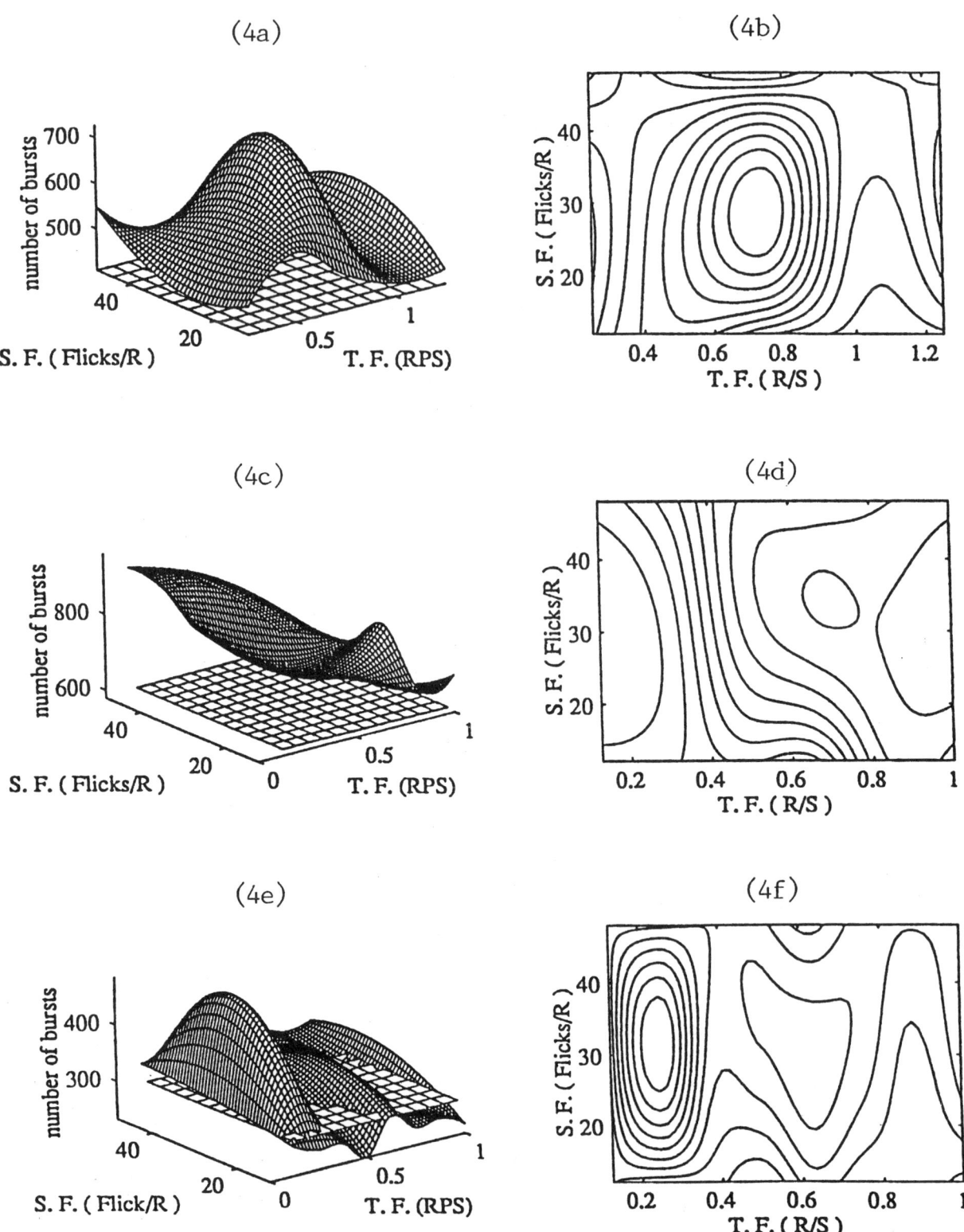

FIG. 4(a–f). Examples of receptive filled manifolds and their associated contour maps derived by an interpolation (spline) procedure from recorded whisker stimulation. The contour map was abstracted from the manifold by plotting contours in terms of equal numbers of bursts per recording interval (100sec). Each figure shows baseline activity (no whisker stimulation) at a given electrode location as a gr-plane located in terms of number of bursts per 100sec.

(see Fig. 4). There are several characteristics of the shape of these maps that are important to the hypothesis under consideration. First, these maps represent whisker stimulation in the spectral ("pure" frequency) domain, since variations of the stimulus are made by changing the spatial frequency (spacings of grooves) of cylindrical gratings and the temporal frequency (speed of rotation) with which the whiskers are engaged. The spectral representation emerges as a "density" of whisker stimulation, which enfolds both the spatial and the temporal aspects of the stimulation. As a corollary, in such a representation "information" about space and time becomes distributed over the reach of the mapping.

Second, the functional dendritic field can thus be mapped as a surface distribution. One way to look at surface distributions is to consider them to be produced by nodes of interference among wave forms with different origins. The dendritic connection web receives inputs from arbours originating in a variety of axons. As suggested by Eccles (1958), these inputs can be conceived as forming wavefronts. But this conception is not critical. When we additionally mapped the orientation of the spatial frequency grating (the orientation of the grooves), we were able to plot neuronal population vectors based on regression to a sinusoid. However, these vectors capture only the most obvious aspects of the surface distributions; all of its subtleties are ignored.

THE TEMPORAL HOLD

What does this concern with surface distributions that map a spectral domain gain us? Llinas, at this conference, and several other laboratories (e.g. Singer, 1993) have tackled the so-called binding problem by indicating coherence among neural oscillators (oscillation indicated by raster plots, see Fig. 5). Periodicity in the density distribution of nerve impulses (recorded from single axons) can be shown to be produced either by sensory input, or in Llinas' hands by input from the intralaminar nuclei of the dorsal thalamus. These investigators have emphasized the temporal dimension of their findings, but, as came out in the discussion of Llinas' results at this conference, it is the temporal binding of separate spatial locations that is at stake.

Elsewhere (Pribram, 1966, p. 179), I suggested that such a "temporal hold" is necessary to:

. . . the flexible rearrangement of memory processes. This temporal hold is assumed to be accomplished through an operation similar to that which gives rise to a temporary dominant focus in the experiments of Zal'manson working with Ukhtomski (1927). (In these experiments they applied a patty of filter paper soaked in strychnine to an appropriate location on the motor cortex which resulted in a shift of a conditional reflex from one leg to another.) Without regulation by such a hold mechanism, the organism fluctuates inordinately among temporal signals and thus produces only a jumble of arrival patterns.

The Contingent Negative Variation (CNV), the expectancy wave of the EEG, was suggested to represent such a temporal hold. Initially this negative variation was recorded deep to the frontal lobe of the brain, which suggested a basal ganglion or limbic origin. Of interest in the light of Llinas' results obtained from stimulation of the intralaminar goup of nuclei is that, with the collaboration of a medical student (McKegney, 1958), I had traced, by way of the retrograde degeneration technique, connections from the intralaminar complex to the perirhinal cortex (as well as to the basal ganglia), an area currently held responsible for many of the devastating effects on memory resulting from resections of the medial portion of the temporal lobe[2].

Binding by way of a temporal hold that produces coherence can readily be calculated in the space-time domain provided there are only a few oscillators involved. When coherence must be calculated over many locations as is done in computerized tomography (CAT and PET scans and fMRI) and in the presentation at this conference

---

[2] The intralaminar complex becomes more prominent as one proceeds from rat to cat to monkey to man. Also, this complex divides the thalamus into two divisions: One projects to the convexal cortex to include the posterior part of the frontal cortex and the parietal, occipital, and temporal regions. This division maintains an anterior-posterior axis, which reflects the anterior-posterior axis of the cortex. By contrast, the other, more medial division, which projects to the far frontal (prefrontal) and cingulate cortex, loses this anterior-posterior topological correspondence. This difference in thalamocortical organization is one reason for classifying the far frontal cortex with the limbic formation. (The other is that resections of the far frontal and limbic cortices produce deficits in delayed alternation behaviour in monkeys whereas resections of the convexal cortical regions do not; the reverse is true for simple sensory discriminations.) For review see Pribram (1954, 1958).

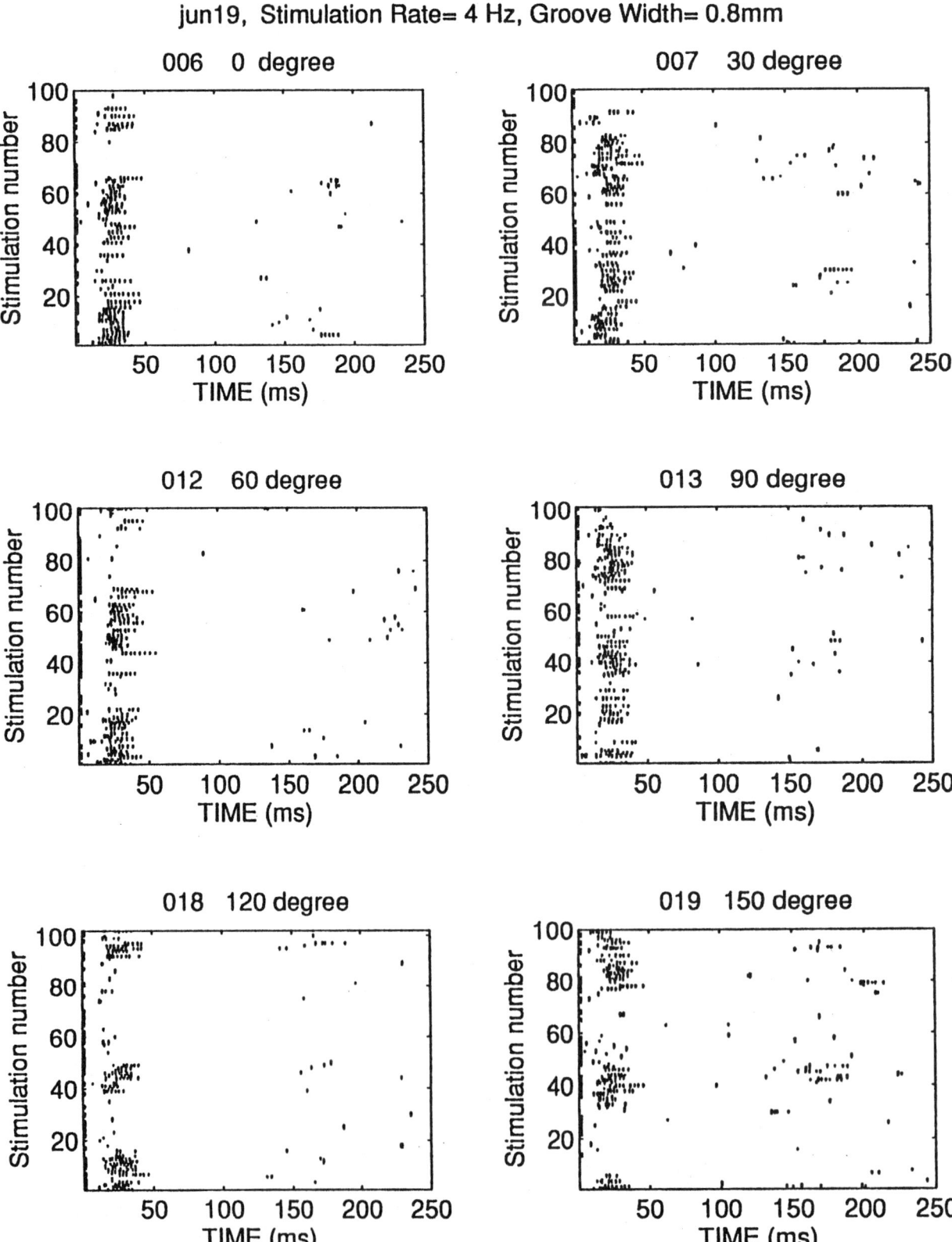

FIG. 5. Raster plots showing periodicity of single-neuron firing as a function of a sweep of a rat's whiskers across an 8mm grating. The sweep was initiated by electrical stimulation (stimulation number) of the 5th cranial nerve at the rate of 4Hz. Although this is not readily seen in this figure, the neural periodicity is *not* identical with the sweep rate, especially when rates of 8 or 12Hz were used. Note that the periodic burst occurs only within the first 50msec of each sweep.

by Petsche for determining different patterns of the EEG that characterize listening to different musical compositions, the computations are facilitated considerably when they are carried out in the spectral domain (by using an FFT or similar algorithm). My suggestion, in keeping with my hypothesis, is that if it is easier for the computer to perform the algorithm in this domain, it is likely that it is easier for the brain to do it that way.

SCAN-PATHS

The analogy with tomography raises an issue that needs to be addressed: We do not perceive in the spectral domain. How is the inverse transform implemented, so that processing can shift back from the spectral to the space-time domain? The spectral domain is time symmetric. What is needed is a mechanism that breaks time symmetry. Prigogine (e.g. 1994) has noted that under certain conditions, the time symmetry inherent in the spectral domain can be broken. He has suggested that under these conditions scattering (dissipation of energy) is persistent rather than transitory; that is, the system is an open, not a closed one. Open systems provide opportunities for a range of possibilities for different futures[3]. Whether Prigogine's formulation is the correct one or not, the important point of his programme is that open systems are open to possibilities. When a path is taken, a choice is made among possibilities (e.g. by the formation of an attractor) such that the path not taken is forever lost, and time symmetry is broken.

This emphasis on paths brings Prigogine's formulation regarding the breaking of time sym-

---

[3] Mathematically, Prigogine's discussion concerns certain generalized quantum and/or classical systems driven by (non-self-adjoined) Hamiltonian operators (for quantum systems) and/or Liouville operators (for classical systems) which are "chosen" so that their time developments are kept contractive (i.e. lose information) and dissipative (i.e. lose energy). My interpretation (Pribram, 1994) of his equations is that damping terms eliminate the imaginary component of non-square integrable Eigen functions due to their evolution operator (e.g. a Hamiltonian). Thus, undertaking a "path", choosing, making implicit or explicit directed movement—whether as attention to input, as intending an action or as thought (i.e. rummaging through memory)—breaks time symmetry. The path taken "loses information" or better stated, loses uncertainty in Shannon's formulation, and, in the terminology of nonlinear dynamics, forms an attractor in a dissipative process.

metry into register with the issue addressed here regarding the mechanism whereby an inverse transform accomplishes a return from the spectral to the space-time domain. Effron (1989) has shown the importance of scan-paths to visual and other sensory processing. Bolster and I (Bolster & Pribram, 1993) have shown, by recordings of the electrical activity of the parietal, temporal, and far frontal intrinsic "association" cortices of monkeys while they were choosing among single or conjoined features, that these brain systems are involved in the construction of scan-paths. Other evidence (reviewed by Pribram, 1960, 1974, 1991) indicates that these parts of the cortex operate back onto the primary sensory pathways to help organize the sensory input.

Individual scan-paths, when externalized as eye movements (which they need not be), do not look directed any more than do the individual "paths" taken by the maximum squared amplitude recordings shown in Fig. 1. But when scans are tracked over time, patterns tend to centre on the more "informative" parts of a figure (Bagshaw, Mackworth, & Pribram, 1970). Thus, on the basis of the evidence that is demonstrated in Fig.1, the temporal hold (as demonstrated in Llinas' experiments) can result in brief "moments" iterated until a pattern of scan-paths accomplishes a percept. On the basis of our experiments and those of Petche's presented at this conference, the duration of such a neural moment to approximate 100th of a second on average (in the range from 5 to 20msec) and that of the temporal hold would be coordinate with the span of attention.

A MODEL

The following example shows how a system operating in the spectral domain can be constructed from scan-paths; specifically, how hippocampal (limbic) function can interact with operations in the cortical convexity to facilitate learning.

The example takes into consideration Jeffrey Gray's and J.N.P. Rawlins' (1975) proposal that the hippocampal formation acts as a comparator; D.S. Olton's (1983) and my own (Pribram, 1971) emphasis on its function as a memory buffer; Abraham Amsel's (in press) experiments regarding the effects of hippocampal manipulations on vicarious trial (and error) performances; and E. Roy John's (1967) demonstration that electrical responses are evoked in limbic structures during and only during early phases of learning.

Specifically, the example attempts to resolve some apparently discrepant findings regarding the results of microelectrode recordings of the activity of single neurons or small groups of such neurons during performances of rats in mazes. The discrepancy is that under some conditions, a path in space is outlined by the recordings; under other conditions, spatial cues appear to be represented in a distributed fashion.

The current formulation was instigated by another presented by J. McClelland and Bruce McNaughton (McClelland, 1996). The McClelland-McNaughton model takes into account only the latter's finding of a representation in hippocampal neurons of a path in space. Thus their model directly matches hippocampal activity with the activity of the cortical convexity (as would be expected of a comparator). On the input side such a model is plausible. However, their model also demands such a comparative process on the output side. This is implausible in view of results obtained by Paul MacLean and myself (Pribram & MacLean, 1953) when mapping cortical connectivity by strychnine neuronography. Although we were readily able to show multiple inputs to the hippocampal formation, we were totally unable to activate *any* isocortical region by stimulating the hippocampal cortex. The finding was so striking that MacLean (1990) developed the theme of a schizophysiology of cortical function.

On the other hand, such outputs are plentiful to the amygdala, to the n. accumbens septi, and to other subcortical structures via the fornix. Confirmation of the difference between input (encoding) and output (decoding) operations involving the hippocampal formation has recently come from studies in humans using *f*MRI (Gabrieli, Brewer, Desmond, & Glover, 1997). Encoding into memory was found to activate the parahippocampal cortex, which includes the entorhinal cortex (which receives input from the remainder of the isocortex), whereas decoding (retrieval) was found to activate the subiculum which (Gabrieli, et al., 1997, p. 265) "provides the major *subcortical* output of the hippocampal region via the fornix".

The subcortical nuclei do not have the laminar structure of cortex and so are poor candidates for the point-to-point match a computer would ordinarily be conceived to implement. On the other hand, a match could readily be achieved if the comparison would involve a stage during which processing involved a distributed stage, much as when a holographic memory is used to store and retrieve information (for instance with holofishe). It is the evidence that such a distributed store is, in fact, built up in the hippocampal formation during learning that makes such a model plausible.

Landfield (1976) and O'Keefe (1986) have developed such a model. O'Keefe (1986, pp. 82–84) reviews the evidence and describes the model as follows:

> Attempts to gain an idea of the way in which an environment is represented in the hippocampus strongly suggest the absence of any topographic isomorphism between the map and the environment. Furthermore, it appears that a small cluster of neighboring pyramidal cells would map, albeit crudely, the entire environment. This observation, taken together with the ease that many experimenters have had in finding place cells with arbitrarily located electrodes in the hippocampus, suggests that each environment is represented many times over in the hippocampus, in a manner similar to a holographic plate. In both representation systems the effect of increasing the area of the storage which is activated is to increase the definition of the representation.
>
> A second major similarity between the way in which information can be stored on a holographic plate and the way environments can be represented in the hippocampus is that the same hippocampal cells can participate in the representation of several environments (O'Keefe & Conway, 1978; Kubie & Ranck, 1983). In the Kubie and Ranck study the same place cell was recorded from the hippocampus of female rats in three different environments: All of the 28 nontheta cells had a place field in at least one of the environments, and 12 had a field in all three environments. There was no systematic relationship amongst the fields of the same neurone in the different environments. One can conclude that each hippocampal place cell can enter into the representation of a large number of environments, and conversely, that the representation of any given environment is dependent on the activity of a reasonably large group of place neurones.
>
> The third major similarity between the holographic recording technique and the construction of environmental maps in the hippocampus is the use of interference patterns between sinusoidal waves to determine the pattern of activity in the recording substrate (see Landfield, 1976). In optical holography this is done by splitting a beam of monochromatic light into two, reflecting one beam off the scene to be encoded and then interacting the two beams at the plane of the substrate. In the hippocampus something similar might be happening. . . . The beams are formed

by the activity in the fibers projecting to the hippocampus from the medial septal nucleus (MS) and the nucleus of the diagonal band of Broca (DBB).

Pioneering work by Petsche, Stumpf and their colleagues (Stumpf, 1965) showed that the function of the MS and DBB nuclei was to translate the amount of activity ascending from various brainstem nuclei into a frequency moduled code. Neurons in the MS/DBB complex fire in bursts, with a burst frequency which varies from 4–12Hz. Increases in the strength of brainstem stimulation produce increases in the frequency of the bursts but not necessarily in the number of spikes within each burst (Petsche, Gogolak and van Zweiten, 1965). It is now widely accepted that this bursting activity in the MS/DBB is responsible for the synchronization of the hippocampal theta rhythm.

The November 1995 issue of *Scientific American* shows how such a holographic matching process could work. Of course, in this quotation (Psaltis & Mok, 1995, p. 76), the matching process works by way of illuminating crystals, and the neural substitutes for this would be surface distributions of dendritic polarizations in somatosensory cortex, as shown in Fig. 4:

Given a hologram, either one of the two beams that interfered to create it can be used to reconstruct the other. What this means, in a holographic memory, is that it is possible not only to orient a reference beam into the crystal at a certain angle to select an individual holographic page but also to accomplish the reverse, *illuminating a crystal with one of the stored images gives rise to an approximation of the associated reference beam, reproduced as a plane wave emanating from the crystal at the appropriate angle.*

A lens can focus this wave to a small spot whose lateral position is determined by the angle and therefore reveals the identity of the input image. If the crystal is illuminated with a hologram that is not among the stored patterns, *multiple reference beams—and therefore multiple focused spots, are the result. The brightness of each spot is proportional to the degree of similarity between the input image and each of the stored patterns. In other words, the array of spots [weights in a layer of a PDP network] is an encoding of the input image, in terms of its similarity with the stored database of images.*

Putting this together with the McClelland-McNaughton model, which is based on data

that do show a representation of the *path* taken by an animal down an alley maze, encoding in the hippocampus may be both holographic-like *and* patterned in space and time. The hypothesis is that as multiple paths become represented in the hippocampal formation, a transformation into holographic-like surface distribution in the spectral domain is effected. When a particular path is subsequently sought, the buffer operates much as does the holographic memory described earlier. Actual paths construct the holographic memory and scan-paths activate the comparator to retrieve a particularly appropriate actual path. Essentially, the process implements a shift in coordinates from space-time (configurational) to spectral and back to configurational.

The shift of coordinates is suggested to take place by way of scanning, that is, constructing a particular path. Computational models such as those proposed by Harth, Unnikrishnan, and Pandya (1987) and by Yasue, Jibu, and Pribram (Pribram, 1991) have been developed for vision to account for the shift in coordinates as a result of such a choice. In the Yasue et al. proposal, Euler-Lagrange equations correspond to *paths* taken in configuration space (space-time coordinates). The shift from spectral to the configuration coordinates has been demonstrated in the visual system both at the thalamic and cortical level. Electrical stimulation of temporal or frontal lobe cortex enhances or diminishes the extent of the inhibitory surrounds and flanks of dendritic receptive fields in thalamus and cortex so that the sensory channels can either become multiplexed or fused. As the dendritic fields can be described in terms of a space-time constraint on a sinusoid such as the Gabor elementary function, the constraint is embodied in the inhibitory surround of the field. Enhancing the surround enhances processing in configuration coordinates; diminishing the surround enhances the sinusoidal (spectral domain) aspects of processing. Thus, the development of scan-paths operates on the inhibitory process that characterize the fluctuations of the polarizations of the dendritic connection web.

END-THOUGHTS

In a way, it is a miracle that we can garner meaning from the recording of brain electrical activity. Imagine what you might learn from placing electrodes on top of a computer to determine which program is in operation (or even whether the program is in hexadecimal, ASCII, or C++). Or, take a single wire and stick it into the guts of the computer (and hope you won't short anything out) to find out in machine language what is going on. Despite such odds, by hard work and, what is essential, by synthesizing the results with those obtained with other techniques, meaning has been harvested from recordings of brain electrical activity. Have we got it totally right as yet? Probably not. But when I think back to what we knew half a century ago about how the brain operates to organize our perceptions and our memory and our behaviour, I can only be optimistic: 24,000 neuroscientists are in the trenches ready to seize the next vantage.

REFERENCES

Adey, W.R. (1967). Intrinsic organization of cerebral tissue in alerting, orienting, and discriminative responses. In G.C. Quarton, T. Melnechuk, & F.O. Schmitt (Eds.), *The neurosciences* (pp. 615–633). New York: The Rockefellar Press.

Amsel, A. (in press). On cognitive maps, vicarious trial-and-error, and impulsivity. In K.H. Pribram (Ed.), *Brain and values*. Hillsdale, NJ: Lawrence Erlbaum Associates Inc.

Bagshaw, M.H., Macworth, N.H., & Pribram, K.H. (1970). The effect of inferotemporal cortex ablations on eye movements of monkeys during discrimination training. *International Journal of Neuroscience, 1*, 153–158.

Bishop, G. (1956). Natural history of the nerve impulse. *Physiological Review, 36*, 376–399.

Bolster, B., & Pribram, K.H. (1993). Cortical involvement in visual scan in the monkey. *Perception and Psychophysics, 53*(5), 505–518. Austin, TX: The Psychonomic Society.

Creutzfeld, O.D. (1961). General physiology of cortical neurons and neuronal information in the visual system. In M.A.B. Brazier (Ed.), *Brain and behavior* (pp. 299–358). Washington, DC: American Institute of Biological Sciences.

Eccles, J.C. (1958). The physiology of imagination. *Scientific American, 199*, 135–146.

Effron, R. (1989). *The decline and fall of hemispheric specialization.* Hillsdale, NJ: Lawrence Erlbaum Associates Inc.

Gabrieli, J.D.E., Brewer, J.B., Desmond, J.E., & Glover, G.H. (1997). Separate neural bases of two fundamental memory processes in the human medial temporal lobe. *Science, 276*, 264–266.

Gray, J., & Rawlins, J.N.P. (1975). Comparator and buffer memory: An attempt to integrate two models of hippocampal function. In R.L. Isaacson & K.H. Pribram (Eds), *The hippocampus, Vol. I and II* (pp. 159–196). New York: Plenum.

Green, J.D., Maxwell, D.S., & Petsche, H. (1961). Hippocampal electrical activity III. Unitary events and genesis of slow waves. *EEG Clinical Neurophysiology, 13*, 854–867.

Green, J.D., & Petsche, H. (1961). Hippocampal electral activity II. Virtual generators. *EEG Clinical Neurophysiology, 13*, 847–853.

Harth, E., Unnikrishnan, P., & Pandya, A.S. (1987). The inversion of sensory processing by feedback pathways: Model of visual cognitive functions. *Science, 237*, 184–187.

John, E.R. (1967). *Mechanisms of memory.* New York: Academic Press.

Kubie, J.L., & Ranck, J.B. (1983). Sensory-behavioural correlates in individual hippocampus neurones in three situations: Space and context. In W. Seifert (Ed.), *Neurobiology of the hippocampus* (pp. 433–447). London: Academic Press.

Kuffler, S.W. (1953). Discharge patterns and functional organization of mammalian retina. *Journal of Neurophysiology, 16*, 37–69.

Landfield, P.W. (1976). Synchronous EEG rhythms: Their nature and their possible functions in memory, information transmission and behaviour. In E.H. Gispen (Ed.), *Molecular and functional neurobiology*. Amsterdam: Elsevier.

Lashley, K.S. (1942). The problem of cerebral organization in vision. In *Biological symposia, Vol. VII, Visual mechanisms* (pp. 301–322). Lancaster, UK: Jacques Cattell Press.

Li, C.L., Cullen, C., & Jasper, H.H. (1956). Laminar microelectrode analysis of cortical unspecific recruiting responses and spontaneous rhythms. *Journal of Neurophysiology, 19*, 131–143.

MacLean, P. (1990) *The Triune brain in evolution: Role in paleocerebral functions.* New York: Plenum Press.

McClelland, J. (1996). Role of the hippocampus in learning and memory: A computational analysis. In T. Ono, B.L. McNaughton, S. Molotchnikoff, E.T. Rolls, & H. Nichijo (Eds.), *Perception, memory and emotion: Frontier in neuroscience* (pp. 601–613). Oxford: Elsevier Science.

McKegney, F.P. (1958). Telencephalic projections of the midline and intralaminar nuclei in the cat. *Yale Journal of Biological Medicine, 30*, 415–428.

O'Keefe, J. (1986). Is consciousness the gateway to the hippocampal cognitive map? A speculative essay on the neural basis of mind. *Brain and Mind*, 59–98.

O'Keefe, J., & Conway, D.H. (1978). Hippocampal place units in the freely moving rat: Why they fire where they fire. *Experimental Brain Research, 31*, 573–590.

Olton, D.S. (1983). Memory functions and the hippocampus. In W. Seifert (Ed.), *Neurobiology of the hippocampus*. New York: Academic Press.

Petsche, H., Gogolak, G., & Van Zwieten, X. (1965). Rhythmicity of septal cell discharges at various levels of reticular excitation. *EEG Clinical Neurophysiology, 19*, 25–33.

Pribram, K.H. (1954). Toward a science of neuropsychology (method and data). In R.A. Patton (Ed.), *Current trends in psychology and the behavioral sciences* (pp. 115–142). Pittsburgh, PA: University of Pittsburgh Press.

Pribram, K.H. (1958). Neocortical function in behavior. In H.F. Harlow & C.N. Woolsey (Eds.), *Bio-

logical and biochemical bases of behavior (pp. 151–172). Madison, WI: University of Wisconsin Press.

Pribram, K.H. (1960). The intrinsic systems of the forebrain. In J. Field, H.W. Magoun, & V.E. Hall (Eds.), *Handbook of physiology, neurophysiology II* (pp. 1323–1324). Washington, DC: American Physiological Society.

Pribram, K.H. (1966). Some dimensions of remembering: Steps toward a neuropsychological model of memory. In J. Gaito (Ed.), *Macromolecules and behavior* (pp. 165–187). New York: Academic Press.

Pribram, K.H. (1971). *Languages of the brain: Experimental paradoxes and principles in neuropsychology.* Englewood Cliffs, NJ: Prentice-Hall. (Previous editions: Monterey, CA: Brooks/Cole, 1977; New York: Brandon House, 1982.)

Pribram, K.H. (1974). How is it that sensing so much we can do so little? In K.H. Pribram (Contrib. Ed.), Central processing of sensory input. In F.O. Schmitt & F.G. Worden (Eds.), *The neurosciences third study program* (pp. 249–261). Cambridge, MA: MIT Press.

Pribram, K.H. (1986). The role of cortico-cortical connections. In F. Lepore, M. Ptito, & H. Jasper (Eds.), *Two hemispheres—one brain; functions of the corpus callosum.* New York: Alan R. Liss.

Pribram, K.H. (1991). *Brain and perception: Holonomy and structure in figural processing.* Hillsdale, NJ: Lawrence Erlbaum Associates Inc.

Pribram, K.H. (1994). Afterword to *Origins: Brain and self organization* (pp. 707–708). Hillsdale, NJ: Lawrence Erlbaum Associates Inc.

Pribram, K.H., & Maclean, P.D. (1953). Neuronographic analysis of medial and basal cerebral cortex. II. Monkey. *Journal of Neurophysiology, 16*, 324–340.

Prigogine, I. (1994). Mind and matter: Beyond the Catesian dualism. In K.H. Pribram (Ed.), *Origins: Brain and self organization* (pp. 2–15). Mahwah, NJ: Lawrence Erlbaum Associates Inc.

Psaltis, D, & Mok, F. (1995). Holographic memories. *Scientific American, 273*(5), 70–76.

Singer, W. (1993). Synchronization of cortical activity and its putative role in information processing and learning. *Annual Review of Physiology, 55*, 349–374.

Stumpf, C. (1965). Drug action on the electrical activity of the hippocampus. *International Review of Neurobiology, 8*, 77–138.

Ukhtomski, A.A. (1927). Concerning the condition of excitation in dominance. *Novoe y refteksologie I fiziologii nervnoisystemry, 2*, 3–15.

Verzeano, M., & Laufer, M. (1970). The activity of neuronal networks in the thalamus of the monkey. In K.H. Pribram & D. Broadbent (Eds.), *The biology of memory.* New York: Academic Press.

Verzeano, M., & Negishi, K. (1960). Activity in cortical thalamic networks: A study with multiple microelectrodes. *Journal of Gen. Physiology, 43*, 177–195.

INTERNATIONAL JOURNAL OF PSYCHOLOGY, 1998, *33* (3), 227–233

Consciousness and Commentaries

L. Weiskrantz
University of Oxford, UK

There are several neuropsychological syndromes in which good residual function is retained in the absence of acknowledged awareness, among them blindsight, amnesia, and unilateral neglect. All of them point to the need in studying conscious awareness not only for an "on-line" demonstration of the relevant capacity, but for an independent commentary or classificatory response by the subject, whether human or animal. The parametric limits of blindsight (visual discrimination without awareness) can be measured using a "commentary key" psychophysical paradigm, and the results may possibly allow an approach to identifying neural structures involved in visual awareness.

Dans plusieurs syndromes neuropsychologiques, notamment la vision aveugle, l'amnésie et la négligence unilatérale, on observe un bon fonctionnement résiduel alors que le patient semble ne pas prendre conscience de perceptions ou des souvenirs. Tous ces syndromes indiquent que dans l'étude de la prise de conscience, il faut non seulement démontrer "on line" que le patient est conscient ou non des événements mais il faut aussi obtenir des indices indépendant sur l'état de conscience du sujet humain ou animal, par un commentaire ou par une réponse de classification. Les limites paramétriques de la vision aveugle (discrimination visuelle dans prise de conscience) peuvent être mesurées en utilisant le paradigme psychophysique du "commentaire-clé" et les résultats obtenus peuvent rendre possible une approche visant à identifier les structures nerveuses jouant un rôle dans la prise de conscience visuelle.

In recent years a surprising fact has emerged from neuropsychological studies of brain-damaged patients with cognitive disorders: in all of the syndromes, robust residual capacities remain of which the subjects themselves are unaware: they are opaque to the patient but not to the experimenter (cf. reviews by Milner & Rugg, 1992; Weiskrantz, 1986, 1991, 1996; Schacter, McAndrews, & Moscovitch, 1988). Thus, an amnesic patient disclaims any recognition or recall of recent events, and yet one can show by indirect methods such as priming or conditioning that the earlier event has been stored. The prosopagnosic patient shows no recognition of familiar faces, and yet his autonomic nervous system clearly distinguishes between familiar and unfamiliar faces. Moreover, the subject can link names to the familiar faces appropriately, and more efficiently than he can to unfamiliar faces, even though he does not recognize the familiar faces. Even in the most "human" of capacities, namely language, aphasic patients can show good preservation of the syntactical and semantic content when tested with reaction times to target words in normal vs. degraded sentences. The subject does not comprehend the sentences nor discriminate normal from degraded sentences, and his reaction time is slowed to targets in syntactically or semantically degraded sentences just as it is with normal subjects. Somewhere in the brain there still lurks a good capacity to do so. Again, subjects with unilateral neglect of the left half of visual space, a condition associated with damage to the posterior right hemisphere, can still show good evidence of processing visual events to which they do not respond explicitly. And in patients with damage to visual cortex, which causes "blindness" of the contralateral hemifield of vision, it is possible to demonstrate that they have an ability to detect, locate, and discriminate visual events in their blind field, a condition known as "blindsight". Even though the patients

Requests for reprints should be addressed to Dr. L. Weiskrantz, Department of Experimental Psychology, University of Oxford, Oxford, UK.

are blind to the events, with forced-choice guessing or other indirect methods they can discriminate certain events within certain limits (Weiskrantz, 1986, 1990, 1996; Weiskrantz, Warrington, Sanders, & Marshall, 1974)

Each of these conditions requires its own particular techniques with which to reveal the covert capacity, but they all share a dissociation of conscious awareness from a capacity. They are also all caused by known or knowable brain damage. Therefore they offer an interesting possible route to the study of brain mechanisms actually involved in conscious awareness or its disjunction. This neuropsychological approach differs, it will be noted, but also complements other approaches in this symposium, in that it deals with *changes* in awareness rather than the analysis of its properties or its electrophysiological correlates. Empirical analysis is usually helped by studying change rather than static states. Of all the syndromes (and the list above is by no means exhaustive), blindsight perhaps offers the most promising candidate for further analysis, because more is known about the physiology and anatomy of the visual system than any other brain system, and also the psychophysical methods for studying visual capacity are well established.

A point that emerges transparently from the phenomenon of blindsight, but is a feature of all the examples of residual capacity, is that one cannot draw any conclusions about whether a subject is or is not consciously aware of events (or of a capacity) simply by studying how good his performance is. The blindsight subject can discriminate relatively fine differences between wavelengths, or relatively fine differences between the orientations of gratings. He does so in his blind hemifield, and of course can also do it in his intact hemifield. From such evidence alone, it follows, one could not conclude whether this is done with or without awareness of colour or orientation. Similarly, from analyzing the reaction times of an aphasic patient, which demonstrate an intact syntactical and semantic capacity, one could not tell from that information alone that the subject cannot engage in conversation. That is, the "on-line" study of a capacity is not a sufficient basis for drawing any conclusions about consciousness. Instead one must go "off-line" (Tyler, 1988, 1992); one must obtain some independent evidence about the subject's state of awareness, and compare this with the subject's performance with and without awareness. In most cases we do this by asking the subject directly whether or not he is "aware" or "confident" (not the same thing, actually) of his discriminative choice. That is, we obtain a "commentary" from the subject. But, as we shall see, the "commentary" need not be verbal, nor restricted to human subjects.

This distinction—between performance with and without awareness—is sometimes discussed as a difference between "explicit" and "implicit" processing. But the point is the same. When a subject is performing in an "explicit" mode an appeal is made, not actually or necessarily spelled out as such, to an off-line commentary. For example, when the amnesic subject is asked to respond to items that are "recognized" (on which he is typically at chance), in effect he is being asked a question about whether he acknowledges that he has a specific memory. This is in contrast to a priming task (on which he typically performs well), in which no such question arises either directly or indirectly.

In clinical testing with blindsight or subjects with related syndromes (e.g. neglect, blind touch) usually the "commentary" phase arises first. It is first determined as part of the clinical screening that a subject with, say, occipital brain damage is phenomenally "blind" in the affected hemifield. Only later is it then determined (and historically this next phase took about 100 years) whether or not the subject can discriminate events in his blind field by forced-choice guessing or some indirect approach. In the course of doing so, one might conduct a block of trials with forced-choice guessing, let us say, and after each block simply ask the subject whether he was "aware" of any of the events. But in principle both the commentary and the discriminative response can be brought together and be made *after each trial*—the "commentary key paradigm" (Weiskrantz, 1986)—and in practice there is a considerable gain in doing this, as we shall see.

Before turning to specific results, some background to the topic of blindsight would be useful. It is not always appreciated that the eye sends not just one pathway to the brain—the often-studied pathway to lateral-geniculate nucleus and thence to the striate cortex (also known as V1 or Brodmann's area 17, or just "visual cortex")—but also to nine other pathways ending in different subcortical targets in the brain. Therefore when the striate cortex is removed in monkeys, it may not be surprising that primates can still carry out visual discriminations (Humphrey, 1974; Pasik & Pasik, 1982). Their capacity is altered both qualitatively and quantitatively, the details of which we cannot go into here, but nevertheless their capacity is still quite impressive, e.g. a visual acuity of about 8 cycles/degree, an ability to discriminate orientation differences of about 8 degrees, and an almost normal ability to localize small, brief targets in space. The surprise is that human subjects with supposedly comparable lesions of striate cortex are "blind" in the corresponding part of their visual fields. As the human and monkey visual anatomy and capacities are closely similar, why should the apparent outcome be so different? It was only when humans were tested in the way in which one must of necessity test monkeys to discriminate that the gap began to narrow. That is, one cannot ask a monkey to tell one what it "sees"; one must give it a choice between alternatives or allow it to reach to a spatial location or to retrieve an object. When similar methods were used with human subjects in their "blind" fields (Pöppel, Held, & Frost, 1973; Weiskrantz, 1986; Weiskrantz et al., 1974), they too could perform at least some of the tasks that the monkeys could do with striate cortex lesions.

Striate cortex is connected to several other visual association areas, either directly or indirectly, via a rich network. But the removal or blockade of striate cortex in no way isolates this visual association complex from a retinal input. Well-known pathways exist, for example, from the midbrain (superior colliculus) to the thalamus (pulvinar) to visual association areas, which remain patent even without V1. This was demonstrated directly in electrophysiological recordings of area MT (also known as area V5) by Rodman, Gross, and Albright (1989) in the monkey. Neurones in MT continue to fire in the absence of V1, and indeed it was established that the route that allowed this to happen was via the superior colliculus. On the other hand, visual association areas may not be necessary for all visual function in "blindsight". Midbrain neurons are, after all, neurons with their own rich set of connections to more anterior regions of cortex (e.g. frontal lobes) as well as downstream (e.g. to the cerebellum). Recently it has been shown that even in hemispherectomy, when *all* cortex in one hemisphere is removed surgically (for the treatment, usually, of intractable epilepsy), there may still be demonstrable residual visual function in the "blind" hemifield (Tomaiuolo, Ptito, Marzi, Paus, & Ptito, 1997).

Through what may be a convenient by-product of evolutionary history, the residual function in "blindsight" is sometimes at a half-way house between total loss of visual awareness and normal vision. Sharply transient events—a flash with a sharp onset, or a rapidly moving event—in the affected hemifield can produce what subjects report as a kind of "awareness" or a "gut feeling" that something has happened, but this is said by them not to be "seeing" as such. They may even be able to locate it and even sense in what direction a moving stimulus is travelling. But for non-transient events, such as slowly moving targets, or stimuli with smooth and shallow Gaussian temporal envelopes, there is no awareness, and yet discriminative performance can be good. And for qualitative aspects of stimuli, e.g. colour, or orientation, or spatial frequency of a grating, or shape of an object, there is no awareness as such even though in all these domains there can be good residual function. It is, as it were, responding in the absence of "qualia", even qualia of which philosophers are so fond, such as colour.

This distinction—between transient and non-transient events in the blind hemifield—can be combined with the "commentary key paradigm" in a way that is potentially of some special interest. My colleagues, Drs. John Barbur and Arash Sahraie, and I have exploited it in the case of one well-studied subject, GY, who sustained striate cortex damage in his left hemisphere after a head injury when he was 8 years old (he is now 40), and has a corresponding total field defect in his right visual hemifield (except for a small area of "macular sparing", a common feature in many cases of striate cortex damage). He has a "feeling" with rapidly moving stimuli that something has moved, although he does not "see" anything as such. But outside the range of rapidly transient stimuli, either slow moving, or of weak contrast, he can still discriminate the direction of movement quite well, even though he has no experience of anything at all.

This was put on a quantitative basis by asking GY on every trial to respond (with the usual two-alternative forced-choice method of psychophysics) by pressing one key if a target (it was actually a projected red laser beam) moved horizontally, and to press a second if it moved non-horizontally. But on every trial he was also provided with two other "commentary" keys, numbers 3 and 4. In addition to responding on key 1 or 2, he was instructed that he was to press key 3 if he had any experience of the event, even a feeling or even a faint tickle. And he was to press key 4 if he had absolutely no experience whatever. Thus, we could compare discriminative performance with his commentary performance. We varied stimulus velocity, stimulus excursion, and also contrast (by varying background luminance).

As shown in Fig. 1, it can be seen that performance could remain high relatively independently of acknowledged awareness. That is, as background luminance increased (thereby lowering stimulus contrast), the percentage of trials on which he signalled "aware" dropped sharply, without any change in performance. Similarly, with a slow velocity, performance could be good without any reported awareness. As velocity increased to approach the "transient" range, the percentage of awareness reports increased, and performance remained good (Fig. 2). Above a certain level when he was well into the transient range, of course, the subject reported awareness on all trials.

One implication of such a pattern of results is that it ought, in principle, to match the performance of the subject when he reports "awareness" with that when he reports "no awareness." For example, in Fig. 3, the results are shown for an experiment when we varied the angle between horizontal vs. non-horizontal movement. The results are plotted for "aware" reports on every trial, and for "unaware" reports on every trial, using different velocities for these two modes. As angular separation increases, not surprisingly, discriminative performance also improves. But note that performance in both the "aware" mode and the "unaware" mode show parallel functions, and actually converge on the same high value, approximately 95% correct (chance being 50%).

This implication carries another: it ought to be possible to carry out brain imaging in each of the two modes, and thus to see whether there is a pattern of activity associated with visual awareness as such. Such an experiment was recently carried out by myself, John Barbur, and Arash Sahraie (for the psychophysics), and colleagues at the FMRI imaging centre at the Institute of Psychiatry in London (Drs. S. Williams, A. Simmons, and their team). The analysis is still in progress, but a short summary appears as an addendum to a book (Weiskrantz, 1997) and a full multi-authored paper will be submitted when the analysis is complete[1]. The main result appears to

---

[1] Results and analysis now published; cf. Sahraie, Weiskrantz, Barbur, Simmons, Williams, and Brammer, 1997.

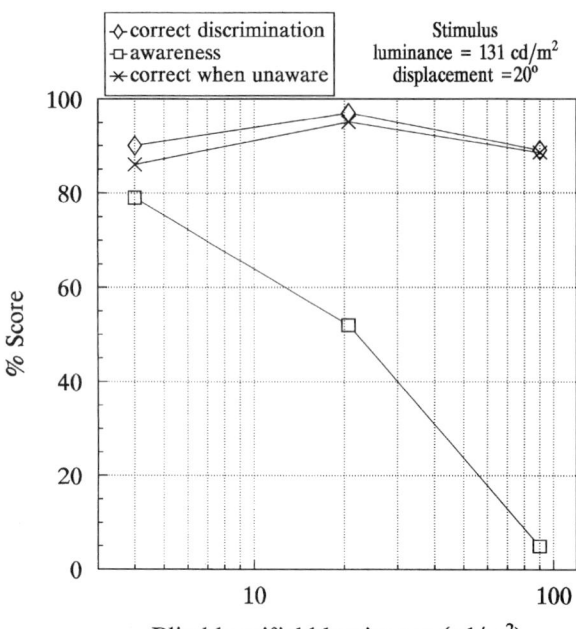

FIG. 1. Discrimination of horizontal vs. vertical movement as a function of stimulus contrast. The subject had to indicate (by guessing, if necessary) whether the presented stimulus was moving horizontally or vertically by pressing the appropriate response key. He also had two "commentary" keys to indicate "aware" or "unaware" on every trial. "Awareness" refers to percentage of trials on which the subject pressed the aware key. "Correct when unaware" refers to performance during those trials when the subject pressed the unaware key. The luminance of the test stimulus was held constant at $131 \ cd/m^2$. The background luminance in the blind field was changed systematically, thus altering the contrast of the stimulus. Stimulus speed was 15°/sec, and displacement was 20°. Note the relative stability of the high level of performance independent of stimulus contrast, despite the steep decline in percentage of awareness responses with decreasing contrast (increasing luminance). (Reprinted from Weiskrantz et al., 1995, with permission. Copyright National Academy of Sciences, USA.)

be a difference between cortical and subcortical foci in the two modes, but many of the details remain to be established.

It was, of course, necessary to repeat the psychophysical determinations for the purposes of brain imaging, because the actual physical environment of the imager imposes certain constraints. This was done. But we also followed up other psychophysical questions. For example, our original "commentary key paradigm" procedure used only two responses—"aware" or "unaware". It might be that this is too crude a distinction—the "unaware" mode may contain some "smidgen" of awareness. And so we also used a six-point scale of awareness. The results were essentially the same: when GY reported zero awareness, this was so whether he used a binary

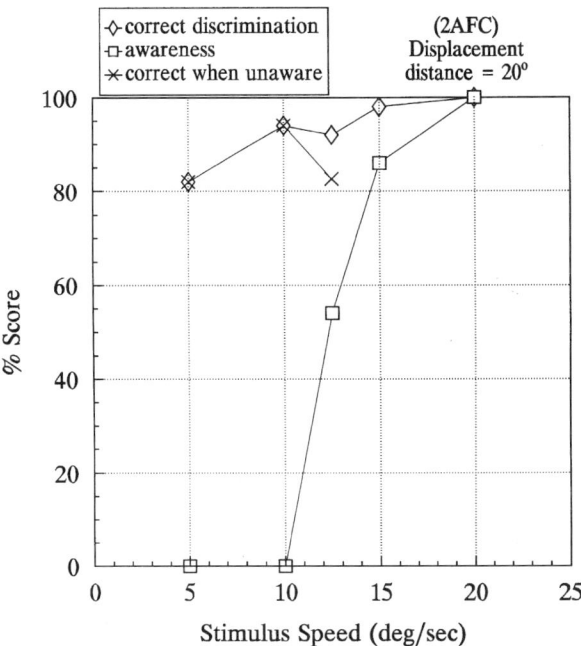

FIG. 2. Awareness and discrimination performance for a horizontal vs. a vertical movement, as a function of stimulus speed, with fixed displacement of 20°. Explanation of key as in Fig. 1. Note high levels of discriminative performance at speeds at which the subject reported no awareness. (From Weiskrantz et al., 1995, with permission. Copyright National Academy of Sciences, USA.)

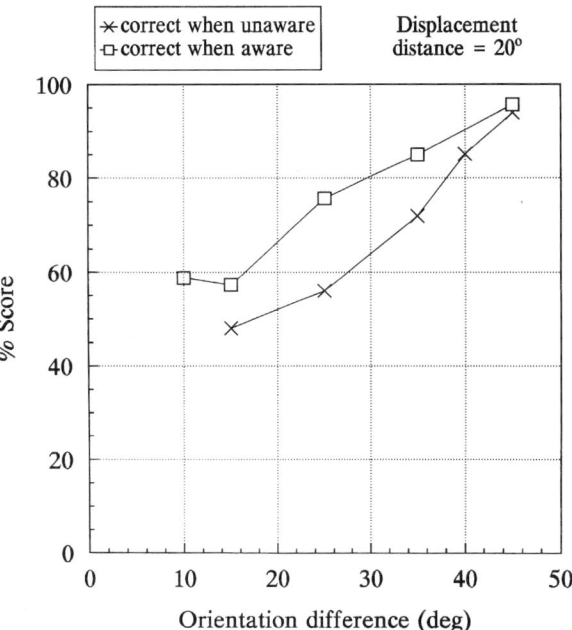

FIG. 3. Discrimination of horizontal from nonhorizontal orientation of movement, as a function of angular difference. Displacement was 20°. Key as in Fig. 1. The "correct when unaware" curve was obtained with a speed of 10°/sec, and the "correct when aware" curve with a speed of 20°/sec. The two curves converge on the same high level of performance as the horizontal-nonhorizontal difference increases. (Based on Weiskrantz et al., 1995, with permission.)

or six-point scale, and the discriminative performance was also unchanged. We also compared "awareness" with "confidence" ratings and found that they did not produce identical results. "Awareness" seemed to be a more direct and useful measure. But we were also able to show that there could be discriminative performance well above chance even with "zero" confidence. Finally, when we gave two extra keys, such that he reported both awareness and confidence levels, discriminative performance declined. It may not be surprising that you can only ask a subject to do so much in any trial!

This is but one paradigm in which "aware" vs. "unaware" modes of performance can be seen within the "blind" field. There are others that are equally interesting, e.g. the discrimination between stimuli of long wavelengths vs. achromatic targets, with varying luminance. Performance can remain well above chance in the "blind" hemifield independently of any luminance value of the achromatic comparison (Cowey, personal communication). A similar phenomenon emerges in experiments in which the cues and targets in an attention paradigm are reduced to the "unaware" level (Kentridge &

Heywood, personal communication). Alternative approaches to the same question of brain mechanisms of aware vs. unaware modes are thus potentially available for brain imaging. It should also be noted that the "aware" mode had already been imaged in isolation in a PET study a few years ago with the same subject (GY), but this was before the "unaware" vs. "aware" modes became uncovered in this subject (Barbur, Watson, Frackowiak, & Zeki, 1993).

Finally, one may return the question to its historical origins. The phenomenon of blindsight emerged originally, as noted, from animal experiments in which it was found that striate cortex removal does not abolish visual discriminations. In the contralateral hemifield the animals can still carry out a range of visual discriminations at a high level, e.g. detect and locate brief visual stimuli and discriminate between gratings of different orientation. But does the animal show "blindsight"? That is, does it treat a visual stimulus as "visual"? Does it do so without "awareness"? The question was addressed experimentally in an ingenious study by Cowey and Stoerig (1995). They first confirmed, as had already been known, that monkeys with complete unilateral striate cortex removal could respond excellently to and locate the position of small and brief lights presented to their affected hemifield. They then proceeded to a second stage of the experiment. The animals were trained, in their intact hemifields, to discriminate between "lights" and "blanks", presented in a random order. If a small light target was presented, the animals were rewarded for pressing the target. If a blank was presented, the animals were trained to press a separate panel. Now the question arises: what does the animals do when a probe light is presented in the *affected* hemifield? The answer is very clear: the animals press the "blank" panel. This is so, not withstanding the evidence in the same animals that they can detect and locate light stimuli. But when asked to classify such a stimulus, the animals treat the event as a "blank", a nonvisual event. They behave like human blindsight subjects.

The "commentary key" approach as a general solution to the question of "animal consciousness" is not, it should be stressed, complete in itself. In the human subject we start with a primitive assumption that awareness exists in the normal state, based on an argument from analogy with our own experience (our self-commentaries, if you will). The same primitive assumption must be made for the animal—there is no sleight of hand or detour around this issue. And, as with the human, we use an argument from analogy with ourselves in a similar situation, but this has no associated litmus paper test yielding a certain diagnosis, especially when the animal and the human are dissimilar in their biology. But when the human's and the animal's "off-line" responses *change* in the same way, as we have seen is the case for striate cortex lesions, the argument from analogy is strengthened, especially when we can appeal to virtually identical anatomical visual systems in humans and monkeys. There are also other approaches to the question of animal awareness, which are beyond the limits of the present discussion (Dickinson, 1988; Weiskrantz, 1997).

The message brings us full circle not only in terms of empirical evidence, but also conceptually. From the ongoing "on-line" performance in a visual discrimination task, one cannot draw any conclusions about the meaning of the stimulus for the subject—animal or human—either in terms of awareness or whether it is "visual" experientially. (Conversely, of course, one cannot determine from on-line performance that an animal is *not* conscious, even if the creature is rather unlike ourselves.) The performance can be excellent in the "blind" field. To find out one must go "off-line." A separate commentary, or a separate classificatory response, is needed. And when one combines the "off-line" with the "on-line" within the same subject, and within the same brain imager, a possible route to the understanding of the brain mechanisms involved in awareness becomes available.

If and when such mechanisms become better understood, this is not tantamount to awareness being "reduced" to their level, and hence disappearing as a phenomenon, as is sometimes advanced by some advocates, for example, of "strong AI". Awareness remains the target of what it is that we are trying to understand. I prefer to think that we should continue to seek explanations that are fully adequate and do justice to the phenomena we wish to understand, "elevationism", if you will, and not "reductionism".

REFERENCES

Barbur, J.L., Watson, J.D.G., Frackowiak, R.S.J., & Zeki., S. (1993). Conscious visual perception without V1. *Brain, 116*, 1293–1302.

Cowey, A., & Stoerig, P. (1995). Blindsight in monkeys. *Nature, 373*, 247–249.

Dickinson, A. (1988). Intentionality in animal conditioning. In L. Weiskrantz (Ed.), *Thought without language* (pp. 305–325). Oxford: Oxford University Press.

Humphrey, N.K. (1974). Vision in a monkey without striate cortex: A case study. *Perception, 3*, 241–255.

Milner, A.D., & Rugg, M.D. (1992). *Neuropsychology of consciousness*. London: Academic Press.

Pasik, P., & Pasik, T. (1982). Visual functions in monkeys after total removal of visual cerebral cortex. *Contributions to Sensory Physiology, 7*, 147–200.

Pöppel, E., Held, R., & Frost, D. (1973). Residual visual function after brain wounds involving the central visual pathways in man. *Nature, 243*, 295–296.

Rodman, H.T., Gross, C.G., & Albright, T.D. (1989). Afferent basis of visual response properties in area MT of the macaque. I. Effects of striate cortex removal. *Journal of Neuroscience, 9*, 2033–2050.

Sahraie, A., Weiskrantz, L., Barbur, J.L., Simmons, A., Williams, S.C.R., & Brammer, M.L. (1997). Pattern of neuronal activity associated with conscious and unconscious processing of visual signals. *Proceedings of the National Academy of Sciences USA, 94*, 9406–9411.

Schacter, D.L., McAndrews, M.P., & Moscovitch, M. (1988). Access to consciousness: Dissociations between implicit and explicit knowledge in neuropsychological syndromes. In L. Weiskrantz (Ed.), *Thought without language* (pp. 242–278). Oxford: Oxford University Press.

Tomaiuolo, F., Ptito, M., Marzi, C.A., Paus, T., & Ptito, A. (1997). Blindsight in hemispherectomised patients as revealed by spatial summation across the vertical meridian. *Brain, 120,* 795–803.

Tyler, L.K. (1988). Spoken language comprehension in a fluent aphasic patient. *Cognitive Neuropsychology, 5,* 375–400.

Tyler, L.K. (1992). The distinction between implicit and explicit language function: Evidence from aphasia. In A.D. Milner & M.D. Rugg (Eds.), *The neuropsychology of consciousness* (pp. 159–179). London: Academic Press.

Weiskrantz, L. (1986). *Blindsight. A case study and implications.* Oxford: Oxford University Press.

Weiskrantz, L. (1990). Outlooks for blindsight: Explicit methodologies for implicit processes. The Ferrier Lecture. *Proceedings of the Royal Society of London, B239,* 247–278.

Weiskrantz, L. (1991). Disconnected awareness for detecting, processing, and remembering in neurological patients. The Hughlings Jackson Lecture. *Journal of the Royal Society of Medicine, 84,* 466–470.

Weiskrantz, L. (1996). Blindsight revisited. *Current Opinion in Neurobiology, 6,* 215–220.

Weiskrantz, L. (1997). *Consciousness lost and found. A neuropsychological exploration.* Oxford: Oxford University Press.

Weiskrantz, L., Barbur, J.L., & Sahraie, A. (1995). Parameters affecting conscious versus unconscious visual discrimination without V1. *Proceedings of the National Academy of Sciences, USA, 92,* 6122–6126.

Weiskrantz, L., Warrington, E.K., Sanders, M.D., & Marshall, J. (1974). Visual capacity in the hemianopic field following a restricted occipital ablation. *Brain, 97,* 709–728.

INTERNATIONAL JOURNAL OF PSYCHOLOGY, 1998, *33* (3), 234–236

INTERNATIONAL PLATFORM FOR PSYCHOLOGISTS

TRIBUNE INTERNATIONALE DES PSYCHOLOGUES

IUPsyS–United Nations Activities

UN DEPARTMENT OF PUBLIC INFORMATION

DPI/NGO briefing sessions are held every Thursday morning, at the UN Headquarters in New York, on different issues of heuristic importance to the UN. Whenever possible and until we can find a permanent representative from the New York area, our UN Activities Coordinator (Michel Sabourin) attends these briefing sessions. Recently, these sessions have dealt with issues of great interest to the pyschological community. For instance, on 5 February 1998, the topic was: "Follow-up to Kyoto: The Connection Between Climate Change and Sustainable Energy". Many issues were discussed during this session that have direct significance for our Project on the Psychological Aspects of Global Environmental Change (PAGEC), headed by the Past President of the Union, Prof. Kurt Pawlik. On 12 February a very important briefing session was held with the purpose of establishing a dialogue with the NGO Liaison Officers within the UN system in New York. The speakers were Janet Nelson (UNICEF), Hilda Paqui (United Nations Development Programme), Diana Langston (United Nations Population Fund), Andrew Radolf (UNESCO), Afaf Mafouz (Committee of NGOs, ECOSOC), and Michelle Federoff (ECOSOC NGO Section). This was a unique occasion to learn the present areas of interest of these different groups in order to favour the establishment of future collaborations. On 26 February there was a briefing on the UN effort to combat global drug problems, in anticipation of the General Assembly Special Session on drugs, to be held the 8–10 June 1998, in New York.

UN ECONOMIC AND SOCIAL COUNCIL

Since the beginning of the year, the NGO Committee on Mental Health (NGO CMH) continued to hold regular monthly meetings at the UN Secretariat in New York and these meetings were attended by our representative, Michel Sabourin.

At the first of these meetings for the current year, held on 8 January, the major focus was on preparing a position statement of the NGO CMH for the 18th session of the Committee that oversees the *Convention on the Elimination of Discrimination Against Women* (CEDAW). After a presentation of the background issues by Jane Connors, Chief, Women's Rights Unit, United Nations Division for the Advancement of Women, there was a discussion to prepare the statement that follows which was distributed to the UN delegates at the 18th session of the CEDAW Committee (19 January–6 February 1998). Of particular importance to the NGO CMH is Article 12 of CEDAW which insures equality of access to health care services and the mental health issues for women who are subjects of discriminatory practices. This statement was drafted by Dr. Corann Okorududu, representative of the Society for the Psychological Study of Social Issues (SPSSI) to ECOSOC, and Dr. Joyce Braak, both from the Gender Perspectives and Mental Health Working Group.

STATEMENT OF THE UN NGO COMMITTEE ON MENTAL HEALTH

The necessity for full recognition of the mental health hazards inherent in all forms of discrimination against women and girls is imperative. All human rights violations are hazardous to mental health. Recent documentation by WHO shows that social deprivations such as hunger, poverty, dislocation, violence and war affect the physical and mental health of girls and women disproportionately.

We recognize that full wellness requires support for both mental health and physical health and that loss of mental health can be as crippling as loss of physical health. Yet there is a tendency to assume (especially under conditions of difficult circumstances and scant resources) that once "basic survival needs" are met, most psychological needs will be resolved in due course. There is limited understanding of the impact of the broad range of risks to mental health and psychological well-being that stunt human development and performance as well as imperil the development of healthy and just communities.

Mental health is more than the absence of mental illness. We call attention to the importance of developing and implementing comprehensive social policies that promote mental health and optimal psychological functioning. We also call for elimination of discrimination against persons with mental illness, as stated in the General Assembly Resolution 46/119: "The protection of persons with mental illness and the improvement of mental health care" (17 December 1991).

Therefore we recommend that the interpretation of Article 12 be expanded as follows:

1. *Call for the elimination of discrimination against women and girls in mental and physical health care.*
2. *Call for going beyond provisions for reproductive care services to recognize the broad range of social conditions that require equal access to mental health care services including education throughout the life cycle.*
3. *Call for recognizing that women and girls who have experienced gender discrimination and other forms of human rights violations require adequate education and attention to their mental health care needs and provision of adequate services.*
4. *Request that CEDAW ask that country reports include information and measures taken in the area of mental health.*

During this meeting, the different Working Groups established by the NGO CMH in 1997 were convened and worked on organizing future activities. The Working Groups thus far established are: (1) Gender Perspectives and Mental Health (2) Life Span Mental Health: Children, Adolescents, Families and Ageing (3) Mental Dysfunction/Illness: Prevention, Treatment and Attitudes (4) Refugees, Migrants, Armed Conflict and Mental Health (5) Substance Abuse and Mental Health.

On February 12 1998, the topic of the monthly meeting was: "Human Rights and Mental Health: A Dialogue for the 50th Anniversary of the Universal Declaration of Human Rights". Invited speakers from the UN were: Akiko Ito and Akiko Ikeda, respectively Social Affairs Officer and Associate Social Affairs Officer, Division for Social Policy and Development, Department of Economic and Social Affairs. Also invited was Eric Rosenthal, Executive Director, Mental Disability Rights International. Everyone agreed that, within the UN system, mental health has yet to be recognized as a criticial issue of concern particularly in regards to human rights violations. This gives the NGO CMH clear direction and a strong mandate for all future advocacy efforts. In addition, the NGO CMH co-sponsored a program with the NGO Committee on Human Rights with the following guest speakers: Dr. Gaston Harnois, Director of the Montreal WHO Collaborating Centre, and Clarence Sundram, J.D., Chair of the New York State Commission on Quality of Care for the Mentally Disabled. The focus of the presentations were "Persons with Mental Health Problems: The Right to Employment; The Right to Community Integration".

The 12th of March meeting of the NGO CMH focused on "Psychosocial Consequences of Violence on Women". Moderated by Dr. Ricki Kantrowitz, Professor of Psychology, Westfield State College, the speakers (June Willenz and Joyce Braak) talked about the "Psychosocial Consequences of Armed Conflict on Women: The Comfort Women of WWII and Others" and "Interpersonal Violence: The Mental Health Impact on Women". At this meeting, the Working Groups also convened and action agendas were put together for the year. Our representative (Michel Sabourin) had previously chosen to participate in the Working Group on Mental Health Dysfunction/Illness. The focus of this group will be the reinsertion of the mentally disabled individual in the community. The action agenda is divided into five significant areas: (1) Stakeholders; (2) Public Attitudes; (3) Education and Empowerment; (4) Quality of Life; and (5) Interventions (early identification, treatment, rehabilitation, housing, employment, recovery).

UNESCO

Many recent recommendations or future activities of the UNESCO General Conference are of great importance to international psychology. In our last column, we had the opportunity to present the complete text of the first recommendation concerning the Status of Higher-Education Teaching Personnel. We must also note that UNESCO adopted on 11 November, upon recommendation of its International Bioethics Committee, a *Universal Declaration of the Human Genome and Human Rights*, which is considered the first international text on the ethics of genetic research. This Declaration "sets universal ethical standards on human genetic research and practices which balance the freedom of scientists to pursue their work in the field with the need to safeguard human rights and protect humanity from potential abuses" (UNESCO News, Vol. 4, No. 7, 20 November 1997). The complete text of this Declaration is available on the UNESCO Website (http://www.unesco.org). On 12 November, a *Declaration on the Responsibilities of Present Generations Towards Future Generations* was also adopted. As stated in the Preamble: "the fate of future generations depends to a great extent on decisions and actions taken today; present-day problems, including poverty, technological and material underdevelopment, unemployment and exclusion, discrimination and threats to the environment, must be solved in the interest of both present and future generations."

More was to come in the area of ethics when, after having consulted several leading figures, UNESCO Director-General, Federico Mayor, proposed the creation of a *World Commission on*

the Ethics of Scientific Knowledge and Technology. According to its mandate, the main purpose of the future commission will be to highlight values permitting better and broader cooperation throughout the world, both in science and technology and in the social and cultural spheres. There is no doubt that this commission would greatly benefit from the input of the International Union of Psychological Science and the active participation of a representative of the psychological community.

Last, but certainly not least, is the announcement that a *World Conference on Science for the Twenty-First Century* will be held in Budapest, Hungary, from 26 June–1 July 1999. This Conference, co-sponsored by UNESCO and the International Council of Scientific Unions (ICSU) "will be a unique science summit and will give the scientific community an opportunity to improve the public understanding of science and to obtain a strong commitment in fundamental and long term scientific research from governments" (Werner Arber, ICSU President, 25 February 1998). The President of IUPsyS, Prof. Gery d'Ydewalle, will participate in the ICSU Task Force for the Conference. The Task Force will work closely with the International Scientific Organising Committee (ISOC) which will hold its first meeting in Paris on 24 March. Two sub-groups of the Task Force will be in charge of drafting the two scientific documents on *Science: Its Achievements, Shortcomings and Challenges* and *Science and Society.* We are also pleased to note that Prof. Kurt Pawlik, the Past President of IUPsyS, has been appointed by the ISSC Executive Committee as its representative to the preparatory commitee of the Conference.

Michel Sabourin
IUPsyS Executive Committee &
Coordinator of IUPsyS UN Activities

1 April 1998

INTERNATIONAL JOURNAL OF PSYCHOLOGY, 1998, *33* (3), 237–241

Annual Report of the International Union of Psychological Science (IUPsyS)

Pierre L.-J. Ritchie
Secretary-General

This report covers the period January to December 1997.

INTRODUCTION

The International Union of Psychological Science is an organization composed of National Member organizations (national societies / associations / committees of scientific psychology, national academies of science, or similar organizations), comprising not more than one National Member per country. Eleven charter Members founded IUPsyS in 1951. As of December 31, 1997 the number of National Members was 62. As a Union, IUPsyS holds membership both in the International Council of Scientific Unions (ICSU) and in the International Social Science Council (ISSC), as well as type-A consultative status with UNESCO. In 1997, consultative status with the United Nations Department of Public Information was established. An application for similar standing with the United Nations Economic and Social Council is pending. A Work Plan for Cooperation between the World Health Organization and IUPsyS was approved by both organizations in 1997.

MEMBERSHIP

Countries with National Membership in IUPsyS in 1997 were: Albania; Argentina; Australia; Austria; Bangladesh; Belgium; Brazil; Bulgaria; Canada; Chile; China; Colombia; Croatia; Cuba; Czech Republic; Denmark; Dominican Republic; Egypt; Estonia; Finland; France; Georgia; Germany; Greece; Hong Kong; Hungary; India; Indonesia; Iran; Ireland; Israel; Italy; Japan; Korea; Malta; Mexico; Morocco; Netherlands; New Zealand; Nicaragua; Nigeria; Norway; Pakistan; Panama; Philippines; Poland; Portugal; Romania; Russia; Singapore; Slovenia; South Africa; Spain; Sweden; Switzerland; Turkey; Uganda; United Kingdom; United States of America; Uruguay; Venezuela; Vietnam; and Zimbabwe. One new National Member, Georgia, was approved in 1997. At the end of 1997, two applicants, Slovakia and Ukraine, were pending approval by the Assembly following a positive recommendation of the Executive Committee. Several others were at varying stages of preparation.

Eleven organizations are affiliated with IUPsyS: Association de Psychologie Scientifique de Langue Française (APSLF); European Association of Experimental Social Psychologists (EAESP); European Association of Personality Assessment (EAPA;) European Association of Personality Psychology (EAPP); Interamerican Society of Psychology/Sociedad Interamericana de Psicologia (SIP); International Association of Applied Psychology (IAAP); International Association for Cross-Cultural Psychology (IACCP); International Council of Psychologists (ICP); International Neuropsychological Society (INS); International Society for the Study of Behavioural Development (ISSBD); International Society of Comparative Psychology (ISCP). In 1997, one new Affiliate, the International Neuropsychological Society, was approved.

VITAL STATISTICS

Number of National Members: 62.
Number of Affiliated Organizations: 11.
Number of Publications: 1 Journal (founded in 1966); *Proceedings of the XXVI International Congress of Psychology* (2 volumes).
Number of Scientific Meetings: 2 Advanced Research Training Seminars.

ORGANIZATIONAL MATTERS

Assembly and Executive Committee Meetings

As is usual in odd-numbered years, the Assembly of the Union did not meet. The Executive Committee met in Stockholm, Sweden, venue for the XXVII International Congress of Psychology in 2000.

The Assembly acted on the membership matters noted above by mail ballot.

The Executive Committee carefully reviewed the new UNESCO Framework Agreement. In particular, it considered the implications for research and special project funding received from UNESCO via ICSU and ISSC. UNESCO's plans for a World Science Conference in 1999 were also noted with strong support expressed for the Union contributing to the Conference in collaboration with ICSU, ISSC and other scientific unions.

The role of IUPsyS in supporting its National Members' contribution to the development of Psychology as a science and as a profession was reaffirmed. The President has written to all National Members asking them to specify activities and commitment to the attainment of this objective. National Members will also be consulted in the coming year on how the Union can best support psychological science on a national and regional basis, especially with respect to capacity building in developing countries and in Eastern Europe. The results of both these initiatives will be reported to and reviewed at the 1998 Assembly and Executive meetings.

Continued support of Regional Congresses was reaffirmed. Following the successful initial effort in China during 1995, the Executive received an encouraging report on the (then imminent) 1997 Regional Congress in Mexico. The prospects for the 1999 PanArab and Mediterranean Regional Congress were more uncertain.

The activities of the several international research networks and projects were reviewed. These included collaborative projects in the developing world (e.g. Child rearing Practices of Low Socio-economic Status Women in Turkey; Social Integration in Southern Africa) as well as those on Psychological Dimensions of Global Change, Bibliography of Psychology Throughout the World, and extending the project on Psychology and Cognitive Science. Directions for future actions were endorsed. Progress on specific projects is detailed below in reviewing activities undertaken during 1997. Initiatives for 1998 and 1999 are under consideration. Several of those retained will be submitted for consideration by ICSU and ISSC. Some will be deliberated further at the 1998 Assembly and Executive Committee meetings. A comprehensive review of Advanced Research Training Seminars also was completed and its recommendations were discussed and endorsed.

A report on plans for the XXVII International Congress, Stockholm (Sweden) in 2000 was very well received. The Executive held a productive joint meeting with members of the Organizing and Scientific Program Committees of the Congress as well as conducted a site visit of the venue. A progress report on establishment of the organizing structure for the XXVIII International Congress, Beijing (China) in 2004 was also favourably received. Former IUPsyS Vice-President, Professor Qicheng Jing, was endorsed as President of the XXVIII Congress.

Officers and other members of the Executive Committee for the current quadrennium (1996–2000) are: President, Prof. Géry d'Ydewalle (Belgium); Secretary-General, Prof. Pierre Ritchie (Canada); Past-President, Prof. Kurt Pawlik (Germany); Treasurer, Prof. Michel Sabourin (Canada); Vice-Presidents, Profs. Çigdem Kagitçibasi (Turkey) and Jan Strelau (Poland); Deputy Secretary-General, Dr. Merry Bullock (Estonia); Members, Profs. John Adair (Canada), Rubén Ardila (Colombia), Derek Blackman (United Kingdom); Michel Denis (France), Hiroshi Imada (Japan), Lars-Göran Nilsson (Sweden), Bruce Overmier (USA), Ype Poortinga (Netherlands), Juan José Sanchez Sosa (Mexico), Houcan Zhang (China).

Finances

A detailed financial statement, independently audited, has been submitted to the ICSU Secretariat. The financial base of the Union is sound although current finances provide little margin for new initiatives. To enhance the best use of the Union's financial resources, the Executive endorsed the Treasurer's recommendation to adopt a two-year financial planning cycle, including multi-year planning for research and special projects. This measure is consistent with provisions of the new UNESCO Framework Agreement.

Secretariat

The transition to a new Secretary-General, begun in late 1996, continued in 1997. The IUPsyS Archives are being prepared for transfer from Louvain (Belgium) to the Union's legal venue in Montréal (Canada). Increased use of electronic communication is also expected to enhance communication within the Executive Committee in the short term and prospectively with the Assembly, National Members and Affiliates over time.

ACTIVITIES UNDERTAKEN DURING 1997

Scientific Meetings

In 1994, the IUPsyS and an Affiliate, the International Association of Applied Psychology (IAAP), agreed to collaborate on Regional Congresses of Psychology to be held every odd-numbered year to complement their respective quadrennial international congresses held in even-numbered years. IUPsyS and IAAP alternate primary responsibility for organization of the Regional Congresses. Hence, IUPsyS was more centrally involved in the founding Regional Congress which was held in Guangzhou (China) in 1995. IAAP assumed the primary role in the **1997 Regional Congress of Psychology for the Americas** in Mexico City with the support of IUPsyS, especially for the Advanced Research Training Seminars (ARTS). Under the auspices of IAAP and in collaboration with IUPsyS and Affiliates, the Interamerican Society of Psychology (SIP), and the International Association of Cross-Cultural Psychology (IACCP), the Congress was organized by the Instituto Mexicano de Investigacion de Familia y Poblacion (IMIFAP) and the Associacion Mexicana de Psicologia Social (AMEPSO).

The 1997 Regional Congress aimed to stimulate the development of psychology in Latin America within the Congress theme of interfacing the science and practice of psychology. The Congress was attended by 2666 registrants from 55 countries. The Scientific Program featured 1500 individual presentations composed of invited addresses, symposia, workshops, interactive poster sessions, site visits, and ARTS. There were over 100 invited addresses and invited symposia given in both Spanish and English. In addition, there were close to 100 poster presentations in Spanish, English, Portuguese and French, and over 60 workshops.

Two **Advanced Research Training Seminars (ARTS)** were conducted in 1997, for the first time in conjunction with a Regional Congress of Psychology. Under the coordination of IUPsyS Committee member, J. Adair, collaboration was received from Professors Susan Pick and Elena Collado in Mexico. Professor Jorge Villatoro organized the ARTS on "Multivariate Methods in Psychology: Factor Analysis Structural Models" and Professor Ramiro Caballero Hoyo organized the ARTS on "Research Methods Applied to the Study of Health". Participants came from a range of countries including Argentina, Brazil, Chile, Colombia, Cuba, Guatemala, Mexico, Peru and Spain. They received a grant to cover their Congress registration as well as for accommodation during the ARTS.

The IUPsyS has been supporting planning for a **Regional Congress of Psychology in the Arab World, Africa and Mediterranean Europe** planned for Cairo in 1999 under its auspices. This activity was approved for a grant from ICSU/UNESCO. However, organizing and technical difficulties have cast doubt on maintenance of IUPsyS auspices. A decision on this matter will be made early in 1998.

Publications

The *International Journal of Psychology* (Editor: F. Doré) continued to be the major publication channel of IUPsyS. The "International Platform Section" of the Journal (Editors: P. L.-J. Ritchie and M. Bullock) continued to serve as a quick-access information forum on major national and regional developments in scientific psychology. A continuously updated calendar of international congresses and conferences in psychology was again part of that section. The Editor, in collaboration with the Chair of the Standing Committee on Communications and Publications, Professor K. Pawlik, initiated a comprehensive review of the journal. This process will continue in 1998 and be reported to the Assembly and Executive Committee for further deliberation.

The *Proceedings of the XXVI International Congress of Psychology* were published in two volumes. Volume One covers cognitive and biological aspects of psychology; Volume Two addresses personality, developmental and social aspects of psychology. Work continued on preparation of the *International Handbook of Psychology* due for publication in 2000 under the editorship of K. Pawlik and M. Rosenzweig. In anticipation of the imminent 50th anniversary of the IUPsyS, former Officers D. Bélanger, W. Holtzman, and M. Rosenzweig have been asked to prepare a history of the Union. A new edition of the IUPsyS Directory will be prepared under the editorship of B. Overmier.

The IUPsyS WWW Homepage is located at <http://aix1.uottawa.ca/~iupsys/>.

Special Projects

The IUPsyS Standing Committee on the Development of Psychology as a Science and as a Profession (SCPSP) completed the **Project to Compile a Bibliography on Psychology Around the World**. Authored by Professor Hiroshi Imada (Japan), the SCDPSP published the bibliography as an article entitled "Psychology throughout the world: A selected bibliography of materials published in English 1974–1995" in the *International Journal of Psychology*, *31*(6), 307–368. A total of 2497 books, chapters and articles were reported, classified into three categories—International: Worldwide; International: Regional; and National; with 157, 203, and 2137 items respectively. Each item was coded following the coding system of 13 categories developed by the author. An appendix table on 'Where and how often can you find country-by-country descriptions of psychology around the world' adds to the bibliography's utility.

Supported by UNESCO through ICSU, the **IUPsyS Network on Terminology and Classification of Concepts in Cognitive Science** has been concluded. Previous annual reports described in detail the project's work and the results obtained.

Previously supported by UNESCO through ICSU, the IUPsyS **Initiative on Psychology and Cognitive Science** completed its work. Professor Michel Denis (France), as Project Director, authored a comprehensive report providing a detailed analysis of the extensive survey on Psychology and Cognitive Science conducted among the National Members of the Union. Responses were received from 31 countries (Albania, Australia, Belgium, Canada, China, Czech Republic, Denmark, Egypt, Finland, France, Germany, Greece, Hong Kong, India, Israel, Italy, Japan, Malta, Mexico, Netherlands, New Zealand, Poland, Singapore, Slovenia, South Africa, Spain, Sweden, Switzerland, Turkey, United Kingdom, and USA).

Given the findings of the IPCS and the potential for interdisciplinary activities, the project will be continued with a revised objective. The second stage will focus on "Psychology in a Multidisciplinary Environment". The IPCS unequivocally confirmed the increasing pertinence of a multi-disciplinary environment to psychology and other disciplines working in cognitive science. The next stage will prepare the groundwork for a large scale multi-disciplinary initiative.

The **International Network of Psychology and the Developing World** has continued to play a role in facilitating the IUPsyS commitment to sponsoring Regional Congresses initiated first with China in 1995, followed by Mexico in1997. Notwithstanding the difficulties encountered in planning a 1999 Regional Congress, the Union remains strongly committed to the schedule of a major Regional Congress every two years in collaboration with IAAP. Other venues are under consideration for the next several Regional Congresses.

Professor Rubén Ardila (Colombia) was appointed Chair of the INPDW.

The IUPsyS **HealthNet**, a network of health and medical psychologists links more than 100 psychologists in 25 countries, most of them located in universities.

As a result of HealthNet initiatives, a special liaison with the World Health Organization (WHO) was established in late 1996. Following a review of the outcome of this activity undertaken by Professor Robert Martin (Canada), IUPsyS will consider whether to request a permanent formal relationship with WHO. A key element will be an assessment of the feasibility and utility of collaborative work focused on a broad range of health psychology activities including the participation of health psychologists in health education, health promotion and related areas (e.g. quality of life research) as well as the traditional area of mental health.

Work of the **International Network Project on Psychological Dimensions of Global Change** on project "Perception and Assessment of Global Environmental Change" (PAGEC) continued with Professor Kurt Pawlik (Germany) as Project Director. This research is supported by UNESCO under the auspices of the Human Dimensions Program of Environmental Change of both ICSU and ISSC. Building on preparatory work completed in 1995, an English-language prototype interview guide and standardized questionnaire on individual cognitive schema, perceptions, assessments, attitudes, subjective risks, and self-reported behaviour of relevance to global environmental change was developed, followed by translations and cross-check translations into the local language of each testing region. On the basis of this instrument, comparative pilot testing was conducted as planned in six countries (Germany, India, Nigeria, Russia, Turkey, USA) with a total sample of 572 interviewees. After data pre-coding by national research teams, central comparative data analysis was initiated at the Project Director's laboratory.

Initial results were reported at the IUPsyS-sponsored symposium on project PAGEC at the XXVI International Congress of Psychology. The project will continue in 1997.

The work of the IUPsyS **International Network on the Young Child and the Family** in 1996 marked initiation of a project on "Dealing with poverty and Social Integration Through Studying Child-rearing Practices of Low Socioeconomic Status Women" with Professor Çigdem Kagitçibasi (Turkey) as Project Director. The research is supported by UNESCO through ISSC. Preliminary work was undertaken in 1996 with the pilot study and the main field research both planned for 1997.

Human development issues in diverse cultural settings were addressed in the IUPsyS-sponsored symposium organized by the INYCF on "Family and Human Development Across Cultures" presented at the XXVI International Congress of Psychology with participants from Cameroon, Canada, Greece, India and Turkey.

CONCLUSION AND FUTURE PLANS

IUPsyS has concluded a very successful quadrennium capped in 1996 by a strong scientific programme at the XXVI International Congress of Psychology, sustained support for the development of scientists in all areas of the world through Advanced Research Training Seminars, dissemination of knowledge in the *International Journal of Psychology*, and sponsorship of Regional Congresses as well as focused research activities through its special projects. The coming quadrennium promises to be no less challenging with an ambitious agenda of Regional Congresses (Mexico, 1997; Egypt, 1999), a comprehensive review of Advanced Research Training Seminars to ensure their pertinence to scholars in the developing world, and the maintenance of a vigorous program of research through special projects. The IUPsyS, like all Unions, must adjust to new funding arrangements with UNESCO through ICSU and ISSC. It will also be pursuing new collaborative relationships with the UN and WHO.

Addendum: In early 1998, technical and organizational problems led to a change in the venue for the 1999 Regional Congress. Planning is now underway for a Regional Congress of Psychology to be held in Durban, South Africa, in July, 1999. The proposed theme is "Psychology in the Next Millennium: Meeting Developing Societies' Needs and Expectations".

Congress and Scientific Meetings
Congrès et réunions scientifiques

June 2–6, 1998
First International Conference on Child & Adolescent Mental Health. Location: HONG KONG. Contact: Sarah Wilkinson, Child & Adolescent Mental Health Conference Secretariat, Elsevier Science, The Boulevard, Langford Lane, Kidlington, Oxford, OX5 1GB, UK. Tel: intl +44–8165–843691; Fax: intl +44–1865–843958; Email: sm.wilkinson@elsevier.co.uk; URL: http://www.elsevier.nl/locate/iccamh

June 4–6, 1998
3rd International Society for History of the Neurosciences. Location: Annapolis, Maryland, USA. Contact: Harry Whitaker. Email: whitakeh@ERE.Umontreal.CA

June 7–11, 1998
4th Congress of International Society for Cultural Research and Activity Theory. Location: Arrhus, DENMARK. Contact: Annie Dolmer, Institute of Psychology, Asylvej 4, DK^a 8240 Risskov, Denmark. Tel: intl +45–8942–4922; Fax: intl +45–8942–4901; Email: iscrat98@psy.aau.dk

June 11–13, 1998
International Congress on Youth Dignity: Coping with Rights and Duties. Location: Milan, ITALY. Contact: Email: unambro@tin.it; URL: http://www.youthdignity.org

June 13–18, 1998
International Conference on the Application of Psychology to Quality of Learning and Teaching. Location: HONG KONG. Contact: Chi-yue Chiu, Psychology Department, University of Hong Kong. Fax: +852–28583518; Email: cychiu@hkusua.hku.hk; URL: http://www.hku.hk/psychodp/conference/

June 19–22, 1998
2nd Conference of the Association for the Scientific Study of Consciousness. Location: Bremen, GERMANY. Contact: ASSC 2, Hanse Institute for Advanced Study, Fischstrasse 31, D–27749 Delmenhorst, Germany. Tel: intl +49–4221–9160–120; Fax: intl +49–4221–9160–125; Email: ASSC2@uni-bremen.de; URL: http://www.phil.vt.edu/ASSC/

June 19–21, 1998
Society for the Psychological Study of Social Issues (SPSSI) Convention. Location: Ann Arbor, Michigan, USA. Contact: SPSSI Central Office, PO Box 1248, Ann Arbor, MI 48106–1248 USA. Tel: intl +1–313–662–9130; Fax: intl +1–313–662–5607; Email: SPSSI@umich.edu; URL: http://www.umich.edu/~sociss/98convention.html

June 20–24, 1998
International Society for the Study of Personal Relationships. Location: Saratoga Springs, New York, USA. Contact: URL: http://www.hamilton.edu/academic/psych/icpr

June 28–July 1, 1998
2nd International Conference: Crossroads in Cultural Studies. Location: Tampere, FINLAND. Contact: Tampere Conference Service, PO Box 32, 33201 Tampere, Finland. Tel: intl +358–3–3664400; Fax: intl +358–3–2226440; Email: iscsmail@uta.fi; URL: http://www.uta.fi/crossroads/

June 30–July 3, 1998
III (XI) International Baltic Psychology Conference. Location: Vilnius, LITHUANIA. Contact: Birute Pociute, PhD, Department of General and Educational Psychology, Vilnius University, Didlaukio 47, 2057 Vilnius, Lithuania. Phone: intl +370–2–762571, intl +370–2–761890; Fax: intl +370–2–622653; E-mail: baltpsy@spl.vn.oosf.lt

June 30–July 5, 1998
2nd Social Learning Conference. Location: Naples, ITALY. Contact: Dr. Graziono Fiorito, Laboratorio di Neurobiologia, Stazione Zoologica "A. Dohrn" di Napoli, Villa Communale, 80121 Napoli, Italy. Phone: +39–81–5833232; Fax: +39–81–7641355; Email: g.fiorito@area.ba.cnr.it; URL: http://www.area.ba.cnr.it

July 1–3, 1998
International Work Psychology Conference. Location: Sheffield, UK. Contact: Kerrie Unsworth. Tel: intl +44–114–222–3268; Fax: intl +44–114–272–7206; Email: iwp.conf@sheffield.ac.uk; URL: http://www.shef.ac.uk/~iwp/news/conference.html

July 1–4, 1998
15th Biennial Meeting of the International Society for the Study of Behavioral Development (ISSBD).
Location: Bern, SWITZERLAND. Contact:
Secretariat: Andrea Kaiser, Department of Psychology, University of Bern, Muesmattstrasse 45, CH–3000 Bern 9, Switzerland. Tel: intl +41–316–313–640; Fax: intl +41–316–313–299; Email: ISSBD@psy.unibe.ch. or kaiser@psy.unibe.ch; URL: http://www.cx.unibe.cg/psy/kjp/ISSBD–98.html

July 2–6, 1998
International Society for Developmental Psychobiology Meeting. Location: Orleans, FRANCE. Contact: P. Kelhoe, Department of Psychology, Trinity College, Hartford, CT 06106, USA. Tel: intl +1–860–297–2237; Fax: intl +1–860–297–2538; Email: priscilla.kehoe@mail.trincoll.edu

July 10–12, 1998
19th International Conference of Stress and Anxiety Research Society (STARS). Location: Istanbul, TURKEY. Contact: Emine Erktin, Faculty of Education, Bogazici University, Bebek, 80815 Istanbul, Turkey. Tel: intl +90–212–263–15–40, ext 1799 or 1597; Fax: intl +90–212–257–50–36; Email: erktin@boun.edu.tr

July 12–15, 1998
6th International Conference of Work Values and Behavior. Location: Istanbul, TURKEY. Contact: Alison M. Konrad, Temple University School of Business & Management, 13th & Montgomery, Philadelphia, PA USA 19122. Fax: intl +1–215–204–8362; Email: V5165e@vm.temple.edu; URL: http://www.biu.ac.il:80/soc/sb/fac/sagie/sswov.html

July 12–17, 1998
XIII World Meeting of the International Society for Research on Aggression. Location: Mahwah, NJ, USA. Contact: Roger N. Johnson, School of Theoretical and Applied Science, Ramapo College, Mahwah, NJ 07430, USA. Email: Rjohnson@ramapo.edu; URL: http://www.skitown.com/isra

July 14–17, 1998
15th Congress of the International Association for People-Environment Studies (IAPS). Location: Eindhoven, THE NETHERLANDS. Contact: IAPS 15, EIRASS, Eindhoven University of Technology, PO Box 513, Mailstation 20, 5600 MB Eindhoven, The NETHERLANDS. Tel: intl +31–40–247–2594; Fax: intl +31–40–212–8222 or +31–40–245–2432; Email: eirass@bwk.tue.nl; URL: http://www.tue.nl/iaps/iaps 15/

July 21–26, 1998
World Congress of Behavioral and Cognitive Therapies. Location: Acapulco, MEXICO. Contact: Laura Hernandez, Apartado Postal 22–211, Mexico City, 14090 Mexico. Fax: intl +5–25–665–5228; Email: LHER@servidor.unam.mx or WCBCT98@posgrado.psicol.unam.mx; URL: http://posgradopsicolunammx/WCBCT98/wcbt98.html

July 25–28, 1998
2nd International Meeting on Psychology Applied to Sport and Exercise. Location: Braga, PORTUGAL. Contact: Jose Fernando Cruz, Instituto de Educacao e Psicologia, University do Minho, Campus de Gualtar, 4710 Braga, Portugal. Fax: intl +351–53–678–987; Email: JCRUZ@iep.uminho.pt

July 30–August 2, 1998
First International Conference on Nonverbal Communication. Location: Bielefeld, GERMANY. Contact: Email: gwolff@hrz.uni-bielefeld.de; URL: http://www.uni-bielefeld.de/~gwolff/Study/conf.htm

August 1–5, 1998
56th Annual Convention of the International Council of Psychologists. Location: Melbourne, AUSTRALIA. Contact: ICP Secretariat, PO Box 548, Malvern, Victoria 3144, Australia. Tel: intl +61–3–9572–4372; Fax: intl +61–3–9572–4132; Email: jd04@academia.swt.edu

August 2–6, 1998
14th Congress of the International Association for Child and Adolescent Psychiatry and Allied Professions. Location: Stockholm, SWEDEN. URL: http://www.stocon.se/iacapap/index.html

August 3–8, 1998
14th Congress of International Association for Cross-Cultural Psychology: Silver Jubilee. Location: Bellingham, Washington, USA. Contact: Walter J. Lonner, Department of Psychology, Western Washington University, Bellingham, WA 98225, USA. Fax: intl +1–360–650–3693; Email: lonner@henson.cc.wwu.edu; URL: http://www.wwu.edu/~lonner/congress.html

August 6–9, 1998
3rd Congress of International Academy of Family Psychology. Location: Athens, Georgia, USA. Contact: Luciano L'Abate, Psychology, Georgia State University, Atlanta, GA 30303. Email: psy111@panther.gsu.edu

August 9–14, 1998
24th International Congress of Applied Psychology. Location: San Francisco, CA, USA. Contact: Congress Secretariat, Office of International Affairs, American Psychological Association, 750 First St NE, Washington, DC 20002–4242, USA. Fax: intl +1–202–336–5956; Email: icap@apa.org; URL: http://www.apa.org/icap

August 14–18, 1998
Annual Meeting of the American Psychological Association. Location: San Francisco, CA, USA. Contact: American Psychological Association, 750 First St NE, Washington, DC 20002–4242, USA. Tel: intl +1–202–336–5500; Deadlines: Early registration June 23 1998.

August 18–21, 1998
2nd International Conference on Methods and Techniques in Behavioral Research. Location: Groningen, THE NETHERLANDS. Contact: Measuring Behavior '98, Conference Secretariat, P.O. Box 268, 6700 AG Wageningen, The Netherlands. Tel: intl +31–317–497677; Fax: intl +31–317–424496; E-mail: mb98@noldus.nl; URL: http://www.noldus.com/events/mb98/mb98.htm;

August 19–23, 1998
14th Biannual Conference of the International Society for Human Ethology. Location: Burnaby, British Columbia, CANADA. Contact: Charles Crawford, Department of Psychology, Simon Fraser University, Burnaby, BC, Canada V5A 1S6. Tel: intl +1–604–291–3660, ext 3427; Email: crawford@sfu.ca

August 24–29, 1998
12th International Congress on Criminology. Location: Seoul, KOREA. Contact: Congress Secretariat, Korean Institute of Crimonology, 142, Woomyon-Dong, Socho-Gu, Seoul, 137–140, Korea. Tel: intl +82–2–571–0365; Fax: intl +82–2–571–7487; Email: cs.team@kic.re.kr; URL: http://www.kic.re.kr

September 10–12, 1998
4th Annual Congress of the Psychological Society of South Africa. Contact: Professor Leickness C. Simbayi, Department of Psychology University of the Western Cape, Private Bag X17, Bellville 7535, Cape Town, South Africa. Phone: intl +21–959–2283/2453; Fax: intl +21–959–3515; E-mail: lsimbayi@chs.uwc.ac.za

October 25–29, 1998
2nd World Congress on Stress. Location: Melbourne, AUSTRALIA. Contact: ICMS Pty Ltd, 84 Queensbridge St, Southbank, Victoria 3006, Australia. Fax: intl +61–3–9682–0288; Email: stress98@icms.com.au

November 7–12, 1998
1998 Annual Meeting Society for Neuroscience. Location: Los Angeles, California, USA. Contact: Norman R Lemcke, Annual Meeting Assistant, Society for Neuroscience, 11 Dupont Circle, NW Suite 500, Washington, DC 20036. Email: norm@sfn.org

November 18–21, 1998
4th International Congress on Behaviorism and the Sciences of Behavior. Location: Sevilla, SPAIN. Contact: (English) Professor Peter Harzem, Department of Psychology, Auburn University AL 36849–5214, USA. Tel: intl +1–334–821–0259; Fax: intl +1–334–821–0780; Email: harzepe@mail.auburn.edu. Contact (Spanish): Professor Rafael Moreno, Departamento de Psicologia Experimental, Universidad de Sevilla Avda San Francisco Javier s/n 41005 Sevilla (Spain). Tel: intl +34–5–4557670; Fax: intl +34–5–4551784. URL: http://www.cica.es/aliens/fcbsb; Submission Deadline July 15, 1998.

November 19–22, 1998
39th Annual Meeting of Psychonomics Society. Location: Dallas, Texas, USA. Contact: Roger Mellgren, Psychology, Box 19528, University of Texas, Arlington, TX 76013–0528, USA. Tel: intl +1–817–273–2775; Fax: intl +1–817–273–2364; Email: Mellgren@uta.edu

November 30–December 5, 1998
Second African Conference on Psychotherapy. Location: Sovenga, SOUTH AFRICA. Contact: Dr. S.N. Madu, Department of Psychology, University of the North, Private Bag X1106, Sovenga 0727, South Africa; Tel & Fax: intl +27–15–268–2318; Email: Madus@unin.unoth.ac.za

January 14–16, 1999
International Conference: Emerging Issues in Psychology. Location: Hyderabad, INDIA. Contact: Conference Organiser, Swinburne Psychology, Swinburne University of Technology, John Street, Hawthorn, Victoria 3122, Australia. Tel: intl +61–9214–5209; Fax: intl +61–9819–0574; Email sbs@swin.edu.au; URL: http://www.swin.edu.au/sbs/osmania; Deadlines: Early registration – 30 September 1998.

April 15–18, 1999
Biennial Meeting of the Society for Research in Child Development. Location: Albuquerque, New Mexico, USA. Contact: Society for Research in Child Development, 505 E Huron, Suite 301 Ann Arbor, MI, 48104–1522, USA. E-mail: srcd@umich.edu

April 30–May 2, 1999
Annual Society for Industrial-Organizational Psychology Conference. Location: Atlanta, Georgia, USA. Contact: Lee Hakel, SIOP, PO Box 87, 745 Haskins Rd (Ste A), Bowling Green, OH 43402–0087, USA. Fax: intl +1–419–352–2645; Email: Lhakel@siop.bgsu.edu

June 9–11, 1999
2nd International Conference on the (Non)expression of Emotions in Health and Disease. Location: Tilburg, THE NETHERLANDS. Contact: Mrs. Tinnie Aarts, Conference Secretariat, Department of Psychology, Tilburg University, PO Box 90153, 5000 LE Tilburg, The Netherlands. Tel: intl +31-13-4662175; Fax: intl +31-13-4662370; email: Emotions@Kub.NL; URL: http://cwis.kub.nl/~fsw_1/psy/conf/emotions.htm; Deadlines: Symposia proposals – 1 November 1998; Early Registration & Abstracts – 1 March 1999.

June 29–July 2, 1999
Joint ITC and IACCP Regional Conference on Cultural Diversity and European Integration. Location: Graz, AUSTRIA. Contact: Dr. Norbert K. Tanzer, Department of Psychology, University of Graz, Universitaetsplatz 2, A–8010 Graz, Austria. Phone: intl +43–316–380–5131; Fax: intl +43–316–380–9808; Email: congress99.psychology@kfunigraz.ac.at

July 4–9, 1999
6th European Congress of Psychology. Location: Rome, ITALY. Contact: EuroCong %INPPA, via Arenula 16, 00186 Rome, Italy. Fax: intl +39–66–880–3822.

August 16–20, 1999
Meeting of the Society for the Study of Ingestive Behaviour. Location: Dublin, IRELAND.
URL: http://www.dur.ac.ik/~dps6jpd/esib.htm

August 20–24, 1999
Annual Meeting of the American Psychological Association. Location: Boston, Massachusetts, USA. Contact: American Psychological Association, 750 First St NE, Washington, DC 20002–4242, USA.

November 18–21, 1999
40th Annual Meeting of Psychonomics Society.
Location: Los Angeles, California, USA. Contact: Roger Mellgren, Psychology, Box 19528, University of Texas, Arlington, TX 76013–0528, USA. Tel: intl +1–817–273–2775; Fax: intl +1–817–273–2364; Email: Mellgren@uta.edu

April 14–16, 2000
Annual Society for Industrial-Organizational Psychology. Conference Location: New Orleans, Louisiana, USA. Contact: Lee Hakel, SIOP, PO Box 87, 745 Haskins Rd (Ste A), Bowling Green, OH 43402–0087, USA. Fax: intl +1–419–352–2645; Email: Lhakel@siop.bgsu.edu

August 4–8, 2000
Annual Meeting of the American Psychological Association. Location: Washington, DC, USA. Contact: American Psychological Association, 750 First St. N.E., Washington, DC 20002–4242, USA.

July 23–28, 2000
XXVII International Congress of Psychology. Location: Stockholm, SWEDEN. Contact: 27th International Congress of Psychology, Box 3287, S–103 65 Stockholm, Sweden. Tel: intl +46–8–696–97–75; Fax: intl +46–8–24–78–55; Email: psych.congress.2000@psykologforbundet.se; URL: http://www.icp2000.se

July 7–12, 2002
25th International Congress of Applied Psychology (ICAP). Location: Suntec City, SINGAPORE.

---

* Please send details of forthcoming events as far in advance as is possible to Dr. Merry Bullock, Deputy Secretary-General, International Union of Psychological Science and Associate Editor of the International Journal of Psychology, PO Box 3970, Tallinna Peapostkontor, Tallinn EE–0090 ESTONIA. Tel/Fax: intl +372–631–6962; or Fax: intl +372–2–451–829; Email: merry@vm.ee

INTERNATIONAL JOURNAL OF PSYCHOLOGY, 1998, *33* (3), 246–248

Books Received
Livres reçus

Braun, C.M.J. (1997). *Évaluation neuropsychologique.* Montréal: Décarie.

Les objectifs de ce livre sont de consolider la formation professionnelle d'étudiants assez fortement spécialisés dans le domaine de la neuropsychologie clinique, ayant déjà assimilé des connaissances en psychométrie, en psychologie cognitive, en neurolinguistique, en neurologie du comportement, en neuropsychologie expérimentale et en neurosciences fondamentales. Parce que les milieux de travail professionnel sont très diversifiés, un effort a été fait pour permettre une large gamme d'approches, instruments et applications neuropsychologiques. Le but premier du livre est donc en premier lieu d'être exhaustivement utile en matière d'évaluation neuropsychologique pour le neuropsychologue professionnel. Comme il n'existe aucun ouvrage de neuropsychométrique en français, un effort particulier a été fait pour rendre compte des ressources existantes en évaluation neuropsychologique dans cette langue. Tous les termes techniques et tous les titres de tests sont formulés en français, avec un index français/anglais des titres de tests en annexe. Les quatre premiers chapitres discutent la méthodologie neuropsychométrque, la validité écologique de ces mesures, la neuropsychométrie de la dissimulation et la neuropsychométrie légale. Les quatre chapitres suivants sont consacrés aux approches Halstead-Reitan, Luria-Nebraska, de Boston (qualitative) et britannique (analytique). Puis trois chapitres traitent de la neuropsychométrie de régions cérébrales spécifiques (lobe pariétal, lobe frontal et lobe temporal). Trois chapitres portent sur la neuropsychométrie de l'attention, de la mémoire et de l'affectivité et le chapitre final conclue sur la neuropsychométrie et les ordinateurs.

Cooper, H. (1998). *Synthesizing research: A guide for literature review* (3rd edition). London: Sage.

This book shows how to do a comprehensive synthesis of past research on a topic via a five-stage, step-by-step process of synthesizing research beginning with the conceptualization of the problem to be reviewed through the presentation of results. It also explains the procedures used to statistically combine the results of studies; validity issues, particularly in regard to problem formulation, study retrieval, and the evaluation of research studies; and techniques for combining significance levels of independent findings and for combining effect sizes across findings. The third edition of this popular book has been thoroughly updated and revised to include the latest information on: the use of electronic technology and the internet to conduct literature searches; expanded discussion of retrieving and coding information from research documents to produce coding sheets; upgraded coverage of report writing that includes APA's new guidelines and recent practices adopted by research syntheses.

Cotton, J.W. (1998). *Analyzing within-subjects experiments.* Mahwah, NJ: Lawrence Erlbaum.

This book is intended to fulfill an empty niche in the statistical toolbox of behavior scientists. Most researchers know how to analyze continuous data from randomly assigned treatment groups of subjects. They also know how to assess practice effects for a single group of subjects given a constant treatment on each of several stages of practice. However, except in the case of the repeated measures Latin square design, they are not facile in analyzing data from different subjects receiving different treatments at different times in an experiment (i.e. in a so-called crossover design). As chapter 1 states and later chapters elaborate, randomization of treatment sequences for different subjects may lead to unbiased conventional estimates of treatment effects and of time-related effects. However, the standard errors of such estimates may be duly large because the error sums of squares include contributions from nuisance variables (such as stage-of-practice effects, when treatment effects are of interest).

Ewen, R.B. (1997). *An introduction to theories of personality* (5th edition). Mahwah, NJ: Lawrence Erlbaum.

This book is intended as an introduction to the field of personality theory. Each chapter is based on the work of a specific theorist (or theorists). Part I entitled "Foundations of personality theory" includes chapters on Freud, Jung and Adler. Part II presents clinically-based neoanalytic theories: Karen Horney, Erich Fromm, Harry Stack Sullivan and Erik Erikson. Part III is devoted to research-oriented theories with chapters on Gordon W. Allport and Henry A. Murray, Raymond B. Cattell and George A. Kelly. Part IV on humanistic and existential psychology includes chapters on Rogers, Maslow and Rollo May. Finally, the behaviorist alternative is presented in Part IV with a chapter on Skinner and a chapter on Dollard, Miller and Bandura.

Jaccard, J. (1998). *Interaction effects in factorial analysis of variance.* Thousand Oaks: Sage.

Analysis of variance (ANOVA), the central analytic technique for experimenters, was the topic of the very first monograph in Sage's series "Quantitative applications in the social sciences". Subsequently, the series has covered different aspects of ANOVA. However, none of these efforts featured the critical subject of interaction effects. The author presents different controversies in factorial ANOVA and the analysis of interaction effects. He thoroughly explicates two important alternatives to classical hypothesis testing: magnitude estimation (effect size) and interval estimation (confidence intervals). Treatment is evenhanded and gives readers the ability to employ these alternatives if they so desire. More complex design issues are considered in the latter chapters.

Kintsch, W. (1998). *Comprehension: A paradigm for cognition.* New York: Cambridge University Press.

In this book, the author presents a theory of human text comprehension that he has refined and developed over the past 20 years. Characterizing the comprehension process as one of constraint satisfaction, this theory is concerned with mental processes, not primarily with the analysis of materials to be understood. The author describes comprehension as a two-stage process: first, approximate, inaccurate representations are constructed via context insensitive construction rules, which are then integrated via a process of spreading activation. In Part I, the general theory is presented and an attempt is made to situate it within the current theoretical landscape in cognitive science. In the second part, many of the topics are discussed that are typically found in a cognitive psychology text. How are word meanings that are identified in a discourse context representations of texts, both at the local and global level? How do texts and the mental models readers construct from them represent situations? What is the role of working memory in comprehension? The book addresses how relevant knowledge is activated during reading and how readers recognize and recall texts. It then draws implications of these findings for how people solve word problems, how they act out verbal instructions, and how they make decisions based on verbal information.

Mearns, D. (1997). *Person-centered counselling training.* Thousand Oaks: Sage.

Person-centered counselling training requires more training and a greater intensity of training than most other mainstream counselling approaches, but until now no one book has concentrated solely on the principles, practices and requirements of training person-centered counsellors. The author has drawn on the lived experiences of both trainers and trainees to demonstrate the potential range and importance of training in this field. Accessible and practical, the material covered includes selecting and supporting trainees, selecting course members, skills development, supervision and other professional issues—essential features of all counsellor training, but of particular relevance to the person-centered approach.

Norton, K. & McGauley, G. (1998). *Counselling difficult clients.* Thousand Oaks: Sage.

Counsellors and other mental health professionals will inevitably encounter clients who are difficult to work with because they do not conform with the basic requirements of forming a trusting relationship and accepting help or advice. Such clients can place enormous strain on those who are trying to help them and this book sets out a range of practical guidelines for the management of these difficult, disturbed or disturbing clients. The authors concentrate on the everyday difficulties of the transaction between practitioner and client in their respective social contexts, rather than locating the problems solely within the client, and indicate ways in which these difficulties can be successfully overcome. Complementing rather than competing with practitioners' own treatment styles, this book acknowledges that not all professionals have access to team-based resources. Providing practical advice, backed up by carefully chosen examples and with a sound theoretical base, this book will be a resource for counsellors, probation officers, social workers and other mental health professionals.

Pomini, V., Neis, L., Brenner, H.D., Hodel, B. & Roder, V. (1998). *Thérapie psychologique des schizophrénies.* Sprimont: Mardaga.

Les troubles que présentent les patients atteints de schizophrénie constituent encore aujord'hui un défi majeur pour les prises en charge thérapeutiques. Sur la base de données de recherche et des modèles biopsychosociaux systémiques, Brenner et son équipe ont développé une approche thérapeutique spécialisée de la schizophrénie: le programme intégratif de thérapies psychologiques IPT. Ce manuel, qui est une traduction révisée d'un ouvrage paru en 1988, reproduit en détail le contenu et le déroulement de chacun des six sous-programmes du programme IPT. La première partie de ce programme regroupe trois modules qui ont pour objectif commun une amélioration du fonctionnement cognitif de base (mémoire, attention, concentration, perception). Elle se compose des sous-programmes "Différenciation cognitive", "Perception sociale" et "Communication verbale". Ceux-ci distillent un entraînement structuré au moyen d'exercises spécifiques qui s'attaquent de manière ciblée aux déficits cognitifs. La seconde partie regroupe trois autres modules intitulés. "Compétences sociales", "Gestion des émotions" et "Résolution de problèmes" qui entraînent et développent chez les patients les capacités à gérer de manière plus constructive leur vécu émotionnel et relationnel, ainsi que leurs difficultés personnelles et sociales. Le lecteur trouvera dans ce livre un guide pratique directement utilisable en thérapie et des conseils pour l'organisation et la mise en œuvre concrète du programme, une revue des résultats empiriques d'études évaluatives d'efficacité, et un aperçu synthétique des derniers développements théoriques au sujet de la schizophrénie.

Rudas, T. (1998). *Odds ratios in the analysis of contingency tables.* Thousand Oaks: Sage.

Social scientific observations are made at different levels of precision. When the data are qualitative, rather than quantitative, the common mode of analysis is tabular. This book from the series "Quantitative applications in the social sciences" uses odds ratios as a framework for the understanding of log-linear models. The author carefully defines the odds ratio and shows how it is a measure of association for tabular analysis. The text is tightly organized, moving systematically from the paradigmatic 2x2 case to more complicated tables.

Schwandt, T.A. (1997). *Qualitative inquiry: A dictionary of terms.* London: Sage.

The language of qualitative inquiry can at times seem arcane and difficult to interpret. This book provides a guide that help shape the nature, purpose, logic, meaning, and methods of qualitative inquiry. Intended as a reference book for this vocabulary, it considers the key concepts and issues that help shape the field. The definitions acknowledge the multiple and oft-contested points of view that characterize qualitative inquiry. The book focuses primarily on philosophical and methodological concepts rather than on technical aspects of methods and procedures.

Singelis, T.M. (Ed.) (1998). *Teaching about culture, ethnicity, & diversity: Exercises and planned activities.* Thousand Oaks: Sage.

This book presents easy-to-use classroom and training exercises that are intended for use in teaching about culture, ethnicity, and diversity. The contributors offer tools for teachers and trainers who strive to increase understanding of and communication between ethnic and racial groups. This pragmatic volume is arranged so that users may easily draw upon activities to involve students and bring abstract concepts into the realm of the students' own experiences. Although there are common themes that run through the book, each exercise is presented as a self-contained unit with clear instructions, handouts, discussion suggestions, and a concise explanation of the research-based concept that is illuminated by the activity. The first section contains exercises that vary in focus and includes topics such as ethnography, time, and disability. The second section focuses on culture and behavior, while the third centers on identity, stereotypes, and personal perception. The book concludes with exercises that highlight the cultural construction of reality.